PULL UP A SANDBAG AND SWING A LIGHT

PULL UP A SANDBAG AND SWING A LIGHT

12 years serving with The 3rd Battalion The Queen's Regiment

Written and Illustrated by
John Russell

This edition published 2016 by:
Takahe Publishing Ltd.
Registered Office:
77 Earlsdon Street, Coventry CV5 6EL

Copyright ©John Russell 2016

ISBN 978-1-908837-04-2

All rights reserved. This publication may not be reproduced, stored in a retrieval system or transmitted, in any form or by any means, electronic, mechanical, photocopying, recording or otherwise, without the prior permission of the publishers.

TAKAHE PUBLISHING LTD.

2016

Dedicated to my Dad, Ted Russell

with whom I shared many a 'war story'

and my Mum, Beryl, who patiently put

up with our ramblings

Acknowledgements

The author would like to thank:

Steven Hodder (Takahe Publishing)
For his faith in me and doing all the hard work.

Dave Cole
For being supportive and supplying
all the photographs and the cartoons that he
stole off me.

Bill Dixon
Who taught me that 'being in the army was a game, but
you had to play by their rules'.

A special thanks to:

My wife, Pam and my sons, Stuart, Robert and John
for pushing me to find a publisher.
(The bruises have now all but disappeared!)

And finally, thanks to all the officers and men of
The 3rd Battalion The Queen's Regiment
who I served with and made this book
possible. Without them I wouldn't have
any stories to tell.

CONTENTS

Chapter	Title	Page
..	Prologue	1
1.	Farewell Civvy Street	3
2.	Give Up Hope All Ye Who Enter	9
3.	All Muck and Bullets	17
4.	The Agony Piles On	23
5.	Choppers and Battle Camp	31
6.	Otterburn and Motorman	37
7.	Internment and Dishwater	47
8.	Cyprus	51
9.	Surgical Spirits	65
10.	Rocking	73
11.	More Rock	91
12.	Somme Lines and Musgrave Park	103
13.	Wedding Bells	111
14.	Blue Skies and Belkin Beer	117
15.	War!	129
16.	Liverpool and Green Goddesses	137
17.	White Cliffs and Canada Geese	141
18.	From Peanuts to Squirrels	157
19.	Bandit Country	165
20.	Globetrotting and APCs	177
21.	Fallingbostel	189
22.	The Beginning of the End	199
23.	On the Piste	205
..	And Finally	216

Prologue

'Pull up a sandbag and swing a light' is a term often chorused by a captive audience when old soldiers start recounting their tales of derring-do, more often labelled 'War Stories'. But every soldier on the face of the earth has a story to tell, stories of great heroism or unbelievable bravery, tales that are above and beyond the call of duty. Me? Well I was a peacetime soldier serving from 1972 until 1984 and I never fought in any real wars. There was a bit of a kerfuffle in Northern Ireland and a disagreement with Guatemala but, by and large, it was peacetime. So, bearing that in mind, I wrote this book with the intention of showing the more humorous side of the military because we witnessed the most bizarre incidents and declared "You couldn't write a book about it could ya!" Well I have, because it would be a shame not to! During my 12 years of service I met a huge amount of characters whilst strolling through the minefield of Army life and you'll meet some of those people within the pages of this book. You won't have the privilege of knowing them in great detail, sometimes you only get the briefest of glimpses. But you will meet them. To know them up close and personal is to serve with them, which I did, in The 3rd Battalion, The Queen's Regiment. The people are very real as are the events that took place. I may colour it a little and wax lyrical but it's all true! If you don't believe me then pop down to your local British Legion and ask a veteran to pull up a sandbag and I guarantee he will vigorously swing a light. Whatever your view of the British Army, I hope you enjoy this book. It's not all about the effort I put into writing it, it's also about the soldiers that took part in the incidents and made it happen. It's not meant as a recruiting vehicle and neither is it a criticism of the Army. It's a retrospective diary of my service plucked from memory so I apologise in advance if I got names or dates wrong. I'm sure Facebook will be full of corrections! By the end of the day it's just me taking the time to put my 'war stories' on paper. Having said that these are my memories and this is how I saw it. Welcome to my world of khaki...

Chapter 1   Farewell Civvy Street

January 1972

The scruffy little teenager stood in the drizzling rain staring into the window of the Army recruiting office admiring the posters that showed rugged young men grinning at the camera. Whether they were abseiling, canoeing or just holding big guns they were all grinning. The skinny lad had the idea that if he joined the Army he too could aspire to look like one of these military icons.

And so it begins ...

The only thing that stood between him and that dream was the man he could see through the rivulets of rain water running down the glass, a man in a smart khaki uniform with three stripes on the sleeve, a man that sat bolt upright behind his desk. That scruffy teenager was me. It was a few days before my 18th birthday and I had a sudden urge to do something useful in my life. But first I would have to convince that bloke behind the desk that I was what the Army had been waiting for. Would I be wasting my time? Would I be wasting his time? I felt that I had stood procrastinating far too long now and the rain was beginning to find its way through my clothes so I opened the door and walked in. The Sergeant stood and stared. "What can I do for you lad?" he asked with a voice that oozed authority. He probably thought I'd got lost on the way to the Job Centre so I told him that I had come to join the British Army. I fully expected him to swing into unarmed combat mode and throw this wretch out of his tidy reception area, but he didn't. (Great restraint!) Instead he looked me up and down, frowned, cleared his throat then forced a smile. "Take a seat son." Normally you say that to someone from Canley and they would take it, never to be seen again. But I didn't. I sat down and the burly Sergeant told me that I would have to sit a short initiative test. This I did and it wasn't difficult in the least. (If it was the Army recruiting figures would probably drop significantly.) "Passed with flying colours!" declared the Sergeant with a rictus grin. Clearly he was impressed with my intellectual prowess. He was so impressed that, in no time at all, he had me standing naked in a cold corridor along with other able-bodied young men. The truth is none of us looked particularly able and few of us had much to boast about in the body department. But we were all young, so one out of three ain't bad. But there we stood, patiently waiting for the medical examination. The doctor eventually arrived and it soon came for my turn to be medically molested. The kindly doctor gently fumbled my testicles and asked me to turn my head to the right and cough. Well, having stood in a cold corridor the cough came easy. Then I had to bend over so he could inspect my bum. Why do they do that? Maybe they look at it again at the end of your service to see if they ran it ragged enough, who knows... I was then declared fit and healthy enough to serve my country. Then we had to swear our allegiance to the Queen and she'll be pleased to know that we did that with our clothes on. After that we took the Queen's shilling and a travel warrant; I was hoping that the Queen's shilling was just a down payment and it would be followed by a weekly wage. Within the hour I was back home telling my dad, my mum and my sister Janet what I had done. Mum put on a brave smile and wished me luck with that one, while my dad looked at me like I'd grown another head. Janet? Well, she didn't believe a word of it. Now I had no military background but even I knew that my collar length hair would be most unacceptable so I sauntered down to the barber shop and had a very smart short back and sides. A supreme sacrifice indeed! I knew I was now different because when I got home the family dog, a cross between Attila the Hun and Vlad the Impaler, attacked me. I'd known that dog since I was a little kid and I considered him my mate but the sod went for me. When he finally realised who I was he didn't even have the decency to apologise! But at least I felt a little soldier like. (Although a uniform and some military skills would probably complete the effect.)

February came and it was bitterly cold, and it was time for me to use that travel warrant and depart. Having said my goodbyes to family and friends I caught a bus to Coventry train station and boarded the train for Birmingham New Street. Now Janet believed me! Within minutes British Rail had me thundering towards Brum where I would dash across the platforms and board another train for Sutton Coldfield. When I arrived at Sutton Coldfield I clambered out onto the platform and became aware that I wasn't alone at this desolate station, there were other lost souls there with me and it quickly became apparent that they too were waiting for some transport to our destination: the Army Selection Centre. This is where I met Dave Marshall who, like me, was from Coventry. But unlike me he retained his flowing locks, long raven black tresses rolling over his shoulders. It occurred to me that Dave might be in need of a haircut pretty soon. We all stood there and we were beginning to wonder if the Army had changed its mind, maybe leaving us in this wilderness to die in the cold wind. Then an old mini bus clattered into the car park, coughing and wheezing then grinding to a halt. The driver announced that this was the transport for the selection centre and invited us aboard. "We might make it," he said and scraped the gears into first whereupon the ancient vehicle crawled out onto the road. At the selection centre the bus clawed its way through the gate, stopped, coughed then ground to a halt. Then a very loud soldier ordered us off the stricken vehicle and managed to get us into some sort of line. It was this soldier's job to convince us that we wouldn't want to go home and this he did by marching along our line calling out "You! Haircut! You! Haircut!" Then he came across Dave. "You! Haircut!" he yelled. Well, I think we all knew that would happen. Then he came to me. "You! Haircut!" What? Me? Clearly he had a sense of humour and was having a laugh...

I sat in the barber's chair and was horrified to see my short back and sides float to the floor. Two haircuts in a week? That had never happened before! But it was Dave who by far suffered the most indignation. Sweeney Todd took stock of his hacking tools and dived in, his arms a blur as he attacked the diminishing mop. Within seconds Dave had gone from Big Hair to Billiard Ball. We spent that first evening sitting around lamenting the loss of our crowning glory and got to know each other, all of us looking like extras from the Papillon film set...

"NEXT!"

The next day we were subjected to more posters of soldiers doing soldierly things, all enjoying themselves and still they grinned at the camera (looking back they could have been grimacing). We were also told about the opportunities that were available in the Army and the various trades open to us. I suddenly had the desire to become a rocket scientist in the REME or maybe a Formula 1 driver in the Transport Corps. If that failed then I could be a formidable killing machine in the Infantry. It was on day three that I had the chance to express my desires when I was introduced to the interviewing officer, I knew he was some sort of officer because of the bottle tops on his shoulders. "Well John," he said, "I see your first choice is the REME." "Yes Sir," I replied, because I felt I could make a contribution in that area. "Oh," he said frowning, "I see you have no qualifications." Obviously he thought differently. Qualifications? Nobody said I would need any of those. "Ah!" he said, with a promising smile, "I see you have the Transport Corps as your second option!" Now things were looking up. But then he frowned his familiar frown again. "Sadly you don't appear to have a driving licence." He made it sound like that was an important issue so I didn't argue with him. Then he really did brighten up. "Ah, Infantry!" he beamed, "If there is anything the Army needs it's Infantry!" Well that made sense. After all that's what the Army was all about wasn't it? "Are you sure about this?" he asked. "It's the tougher option but the Infantry always needs good men." To be honest, I wasn't very sure about it and I could still go home, no obligation. Then I ran my fingers through the bristles on my head and thought to myself "I can't go home looking like this!" So I told him "Yes, without a doubt Sir!" At this point he went into a long, rambling description of life in the Infantry. "It's tough. One day you could be in a trench, up to your armpits in stagnant water while other days you could be marching in the insufferable heat of the desert. You may find yourself in a battle situation with bullets passing within inches of your body and you may find yourself shitting enough bricks to build a barracks. Either way you'll stare death in the face and spit in his eye and that's before breakfast!" Boy, he certainly painted a worrying picture of life in the modern Army. "Is that really what you want?" he asked. Again my thoughts turned to my bristles. Of course it wasn't what I really wanted. But I managed to convince the officer that, yes, it was what I really, really wanted. He stood up and congratulated me on my new career and told me that it wasn't really that bad. He was right, it was worse! Some of the lads were a little disappointed with the outcome and went home. For the rest of us it was another travel warrant and we headed off to Bassingbourn in Hertfordshire. The train trundled along and seemed to take a lifetime getting us there but as long as the buffet car remained open we would survive...

Chapter 2   Give up Hope all Ye who Enter...

February 1972

Bassingbourn near Royston in Hertfordshire. When I imagined the place I thought of fluffy clouds and quaint country lanes bordered by green rolling fields. So I was more than a little surprised to find myself on a WW2 airfield, a drab airfield at that. I felt like I was in an open prison. But I did take the Queen's shilling and I did promise to protect her and all her heirs so I suppose I should at least learn how to handle this mammoth task; if I fail she might want her shilling back. Day one wasn't too bad, we took a trip to the stores and signed for our sheets, mattresses, pillows and four poster beds then hauled all of it back to the barrack room like pack mules. Once there, we collapsed into our own individual heaps until two Corporals came along and introduced themselves to us. We could tell that they were impressed with this new intake of fine men by the way they sneered at us. They kindly informed us that they would be hounding us from breakfast until arse'ole time. The latter, I believe, is about 23:59 hours, but I could be wrong.

We were disappointed to find that there would be no maid coming around in the morning to make our beds, we had to do that ourselves. Easy enough I thought. And of course I thought wrongly. There was no throwing the blankets back on and tucking them in, no, no, no. Everything had to be folded very carefully and neatly into what they called a 'bed-box'. They demonstrated it very well and the finished item was something to behold. Needless to say that our attempts were a lot different with most of them looking like busted fig rolls. It was even worse after the sheets had been slept in, all wrinkled and creased. I felt sure that practice would make perfect...

The first night in Bassingbourn was pleasantly spent in the NAAFI where we got to know each other. There was myself, Dave Marshall, John Gibbs, Pete, Sherrif and Forsythe. There were also many others who I may recall as I go along. Dave was getting over the trauma of having his hair stuffed into mattresses. John Gibbs had served previously but I can't remember if it was the TA or the regulars. Pete was a very likeable lad from Manchester and was a close friend while I was in training. Sherrif was a gangly figure who was doing his basic training with us but would later join the veterinary corps. And Forsythe, well he was Forsythe, a Geordie who was very loud but very funny. He could also be very aggressive! By the end of the night we all realised that we had only one thing in common: we were to all suffer dearly.

Sergeant Hogg. RRF.

Day two. Sorry, but I lose track of days from here on. The day began like all of our days would from now on with the training Sergeant bounding into the room at some ungodly hour and banging a broom handle on the end of our metal bed frames. If that didn't wake you up then it was assumed that you had suffered the most massive heart attack and died. In that case you would be propped up on parade until a medic came along and pronounced you dead. This beast of a man was Sergeant Hogg. Yes, that really was his name, an angry looking Sergeant from the Fusiliers with an equally angry looking hackle on his beret. He had little piggy eyes and a mouthful of crocodile teeth and he was a Geordie. Once we were half dressed he chased us to the stores where we would be issued with all the equipment required to fight a war. Shirts, trousers, webbing, underwear, socks, mess tins, kit bags, berets, boots, long johns, gaiters, helmets, tons more and a suitcase to put it all in. I just hope it's a big suitcase. Sergeant Hogg placed us in the hands of the storeman. "Move along the counter," said Sergeant Hogg, "If you know your size then tell the storeman. If you don't know your size the storeman will tell you!" The storeman, possibly related to the Addams family, would stare at the body in front of him and, after a short pause he would burst into his act. "Beret! Six and seven eighths! Shirt! Fifteen collar! Tunic! Forty chest!" And so on and so forth. As he called all this out the assistant storemen leapt around the shelving like demented chimps throwing kit across the room until everyone had lots of everything. It was like Christmas in an asylum. Then we were chased back to the barrack room and threw on our new wardrobe. (Well you have to, don't you?) It wasn't just me, it was everyone. None of our kit seemed to fit. When the storeman weighed me up he must have been looking at the big bloke next to me, perhaps he was cross-eyed and we didn't notice. We all looked around at each other and decided that we looked like victims of an army and navy store avalanche. Three blokes could have climbed into my trousers and marched around together, while another one of the lads put on his '3 sizes too small' shirt and looked like the Incredible Hulk in mid-metamorphosis. One of them bravely tried on his vest but had to be cut out of it, a prisoner of his own vest - imagine that. In the end we all passed stuff around the room until most of us had something that nearly fitted. There was a rumour that someone arrived at Bassingbourn and all his uniform fitted. Word has it that he was discharged for being deformed. Once we had become acquainted with our new clothes, the NCOs demonstrated how we should iron them. Who would have thought that those rugged men on the posters spent time ironing? We all watched as the corporals ran the steam iron over a pair of trousers and a shirt leaving a crease as sharp as a razor. Then we were told that the Army were never happy with shiny boots. They had to be super shiny so that we could shave our faces in the mirror-like toe caps. This was achieved by using decent boot polish and working it with a yellow duster, going in ever decreasing circles until your finger went dead. Then a little spit and more circles. Having spent the night pressing and bulling we were awoken next morning by the familiar broom handle on the metal bed frame and after making our bed boxes, which were still looking like fig rolls, we went on a run. Because the Army were big on fitness they felt that this was pretty important, so we were all marched onto the airfield and made to run. And run and run and run. They told me it would make me into a fine soldier and a champion amongst men. I told them it made me feel sick. My lungs were burning and bursting and my face was awash with snot and phlegm. I suppose when I can do this and grin at the same time then I'll be on one of those recruiting posters. Obviously they'll airbrush the snot and phlegm out. We were so knackered at the end of it we could only flop on the grass and have a cigarette...

"But Sarge, it's only 4 o'clock!"

We did an awful lot of running at Bassingbourn but there were other skills to be learnt so a lot of time was spent in the classroom where we learned about map reading, target recognition, field craft, weapon theory and how to catch bullets in our teeth. It was during one of these lessons that we were introduced to the 7.62 self-loading rifle (SLR). They told us it was a high velocity weapon and taught us how to handle it safely, things like placing the butt in the shoulder and not the muzzle. The instructors told us that this weapon would be our 'best friend'. I could only hope that me and my best friend got on if we were going to share my career together.

It wasn't long before we were all marched off to the arms kote where we were formally introduced to our weapons. Soon we stood on the 30 metre range with our new-found friends, so now was the time to find out if we were compatible. With an SLR in one hand and a magazine of 3 rounds in the other we waited with great anticipation. The first lad got called forward and took the prone position on the firing point where the instructor ordered him to load. "3 rounds in your own time, go on!" shouted the instructor. The weapon was cocked and the weapon was sighted on the target. Blam! Blam! Blam! The soldier stood up, cleared his weapon then re-joined us. "Wow!" I said to him, "How did that feel?" "Just like firing a shotgun," he replied. Well, that didn't enlighten me much; I'd never fired a shotgun! It wasn't long before I took my place on the firing point. I placed the magazine on the weapon, cocked it and awaited the command. "3 rounds in your own time, go on!" said the voice behind me. I flicked the safety catch off, lined the sights up on the target and squeezed the trigger. Bloody 'ell! Not only did the bang frighten the living shit out of me but the recoil very nearly blew my skinny little shoulder blade off! What a wheeze. I fired 2 more rounds, stood up, picked my arm up off the floor and re-joined the ranks. That night I nursed my bruised shoulder in the NAAFI but, hey, that's what friends are for...

There was lots of firing after that so your shoulder slowly took on the shape of the rifle butt and became rather comfortable. In between all of that firing there was more running. Then all of this fitness training took a sinister turn. With the sound of a broom handle banging on a metal bed frame ringing in our ears we were all marched into one of the hangars. The structure appeared to be a hangar but once inside you quickly realised it was a massive gym. Inside lurked a mean looking assault course, a cold swimming pool, a boxing ring and lots of dangling ropes. The swimming pool caused me some concern, I was never into that kind of malarkey, otherwise I would have joined the Navy. But I was thrown in anyway and had to swim a length, which I managed with some doggy paddling and some crafty footwork pushing myself up off the bottom. After all, this was the Army wasn't it? How much water would we see in our lifetime?

The indoor assault course was a deceptive contraption. It started at ground floor level then, after several obstacles, finished on a raised platform some 30 feet in the air. At that point they expected you to jump off on to a giant mattress that had seen better days. (I did notice that none of the instructors demonstrated this feat!) I ran at the first obstacle and clambered up, making slow progress towards the dreaded drop. But, ahead of me, I couldn't help but notice the figure on the platform ahead, frozen and not too keen to jump. "Push him orf!" shouted an instructor from the safety of the floor below. Two things crossed my mind. Firstly, the bloke ahead of me was somewhat bigger than me and he might just seek revenge later by ripping me a new arse 'ole. Secondly, if I paused long enough I might not want to take the leap of faith myself. So I just ran past him and went off the end, landing on the old mattress which gave a loud gasp. The lad who wouldn't jump? I don't know, but I do know I was still alive and retained my original arse 'ole. The dangling ropes were fun really, climb up, touch the top bar and come down again. The sort of thing I did at school lots of times. Although most of us found it easy, John Gibbs didn't. It may have been that he didn't have a head for heights or he couldn't grip the rope. Either way he was still groping the rope with his feet firmly planted on the ground when the rest of us were taking a shower.

The day came when we had to enter the boxing ring. Now I didn't mind chinning someone if they upset me but I didn't think I could punch someone because I was told to. So I got paired off with my mate Pete, from Manchester. Together we devised a plan so that we would both exit the ring unscathed. We only had a minute in the ring so we would fart about with some fancy footwork, throw a couple of half-hearted punches and walk away with our pride intact. We both thought that was a good idea and sealed the deal. My physical training instructor called me into my corner and Pete's to his. "Right!" said my instructor, "See that piece of shit in that corner?" "Who?" I said, "My mate Pete?" The veins in my PTIs neck bulged. "He's not your mate!" he hissed through gritted teeth, "He's the enemy! He's a piece of worthless shit! You'll go out there, kill him and bring his body back for a trophy!" "Right you are."

I said, knowing full well that me and Pete had a foolproof plan. The bell rang and we came out of our corners. I did some impressive footwork looking like Max Wall while Pete charged over and punched me square between the eyes. Shit! He must have killed a shed full of brain cells before I realised our 'foolproof' plan had been ditched. Obviously his instructor was more motivating than mine. After a very long minute the bell rang and I climbed out of the ring looking like the elephant man. But we were still mates. We had to be, I didn't want to fall out with him too often. We sat in the NAAFI that night and laughed at the events of the day. Pete laughed until his sides hurt. I laughed until my teeth hurt...

Chapter 3   All Muck and Bullets

Training was all about early morning starts and late night finishing. Sleep seemed to be something that eluded most of us. Being an airfield, Bassingbourn lent itself well to whipping young recruits into shape; whether you were running your heart out or recreating the battle of the Somme, it had it all. Camouflage came under field craft and we had much to learn about on that subject. We were all marched out into the wilderness at the rear of the camp and formed up facing a small copse. One of the NCOs explained the advantage of concealment. "If the enemy can't see you he can't shoot you!" That caught my attention so I thought I would hang on to his every word because this sounded useful. Then he indicated the wooded area to our front and invited us to 'spot the squaddie'. We all peered at the trees hoping to spot someone, anyone, so we could earn some brownie points. But no, apart from trees we couldn't see anything. Then the NCO blew on his whistle and we were all suitably astounded when three bushes walked out of the tree line. Very impressive. We were then given the opportunity to emulate these military icons.

"First prize to Carmen Miranda here."

Off we toddled, pulling out all the fauna we could lay our hands on, like a swarm of locusts stripping the land bare. I tried to rip a tree from its roots figuring I could hide behind it at any given moment but that wasn't allowed. At the end of the harvesting we all stood there awaiting the inspection and the inevitable praise that would follow.

The inspection came without delay but the praise would be somewhat longer. "What a shower of shit!" remarked Sergeant Hogg as he walked along our ragged line. Clearly there was more to this flower arranging than met the eye. More work required in that department...

Practical map reading was a barrel of laughs. It comes under 'How to get lost in a professional manner'. And we did get lost. If they had asked us to find a pub it wouldn't have been a problem but they wanted us to find a grid reference in the dark. Then you have to use a compass taking into account bearings, back bearings, ball bearings, true north and magnetic north! Being naïve, I thought there was only one north. With heavy hearts we set off in groups of three, slowly melting into the darkness. And that's another problem, three blokes with three different idea of where they were going! To be honest, at that stage, if I had set off on my own I would still be wandering around Bassingbourn now. All we had to do was locate an NCO who would be waiting at a pre-determined grid reference. Now that was another thing which compounded the problem, he wouldn't let you know he was there unless you trod on him. After such a wonderful night out in the wilds we returned to our beds at 3 in the morning and awaited the broom handle on the metal bed frame...

There were more hours spent on the ranges, converting taxpayers' money into empty cases. (Fear not, we always picked up the brass - and we were taxpayers too!) We actually got to a stage where we could hit the targets. That was live firing on the Barton ranges, but a lot of our exercises were performed firing blanks. Now don't be fooled into thinking that blanks are harmless, because they're not. It's a case that has wadding in the front of it to stop the powder charge from spilling out and it's the wadding that leaves the end of the barrel. I recall one day we were on the Close Quarter Battle (CQB) range. John Curry was a great lad from Brum, and it was he and I that fought our way through the range. We leapt from building to building firing blanks like they were going out of fashion. We did this enthusiastically until one of the 'enemy' popped up and shot John in the leg at close range. Well, while John lay there squealing in agony we all inspected his wound. His trouser leg was perforated like a tea bag and when we looked at his leg it was much the same. The NCO in charge detailed me to take him to the medical centre so off we went, with John clinging to me like his life depended on it. After dragging my wounded comrade half a mile we finally made it to the sick bay. There a medical orderly, who had seen more than his fair share of malingerers, looked at us with disdain. "What's up with him then?" he asked tersely. "Shot in the leg." I told him. Well, this medic went off like shit off a shovel and white coated personnel came racing out of the woodwork, a lot like the cockroaches in the cookhouse. The reception area soon looked like a makeshift operating theatre. They hoisted the groaning John onto a trolley and started cutting his trouser leg open. John groaned some more. "What calibre?" asked someone. "7.62." I said, because I knew these technical things! They all peered at John's mortal wound then everything ground to a halt. "7.62 what?" asked an officer through his surgical mask. "Blank," I replied. Well did they look pissed off! It might not seem much to him but we thought it was worth a plaster at least.

Although I found the physical side of training a struggle I managed to cope. Other recruits had an Achilles heel of some sort or another, like John Gibbs. He was a wonderful bloke and most of the training came relatively easy to him but he still had a problem with those ropes. While everyone else was touching the top bar he was still two inches off the floor breaking into a serious sweat. He could only hope there weren't too many ropes between now and the end of his career.

Meanwhile we were about to leave the barracks and head off to the Stanford training area. Stanford was a huge place full of trees, rivers and lots of mud. The neighbourhood assault course had the deceptive name of 'Evergreen' or something similar. In fact it was a meandering course of obstacles through a track of black mud. Wonderful. We felt the platoon was becoming a formidable fighting machine now (although Sergeant Hogg had a different opinion) and we prepared ourselves for the assault course. With our loins girded we rushed forward to the first obstacle with enthusiasm never before seen in these parts. By the time we got to the second bit, our enthusiasm waned a tad. In fact, to be honest, it had well and truly disappeared. Then came the 8 foot wall. Not too big a deal, two of the tallest lads would position themselves at the base of the wall and when the first body approached they would grab him by the boots and push him skyward whereupon he would grab the top ledge and haul himself over. This was repeated until the whole platoon was over. Having seen it done I ran to the wall and the platoon heavies propelled me upward where I managed to grab the top. But I found a problem hauling myself over it; the weight of my back-pack wouldn't let me. Fine, I thought, I'll just drop down again and rethink it through. But I couldn't do that either because my ammo pouches sat tightly on the ledge. So I hung there like a muppet.

Eventually the two tall blokes came over the wall and gave me a welcome pull. Next we came up against the cargo net and, as luck would have it, I got over that very quickly. This was because as I clambered up the net the big bloke in front was just going over the top. As he went down the other side his weight caused the net to shift which took me over the top rail. I casually climbed down and continued on. Life can be so forgiving sometimes. Further along we met the rope swing, a soggy bit of very old rope dangling over a pit of that black mud I mentioned earlier. One by one we swung over and landed on the other side with a sigh of relief.

John Gibbs never did like ropes ...

John Gibbs was just ahead of me and the soggy rope was swung towards him. He grabbed it, took a deep breath then launched himself. That bit went well but, about half way through the swing, his hands slipped down the rope where he majestically sank into the black shit, a tsunami of black treacle marking his descent. I couldn't bring myself to laugh because I knew that we had a river crossing coming up that night and you know how much I love the water...

It was dark and raining. We were all knackered so we weren't happy standing on the river bank staring at the fast flowing water in front of us. Especially me. With all of our weapons and kit we had to make our way to the opposite bank, a bank we couldn't even see in the darkness. I did notice a perfectly serviceable bridge less than a hundred yards away but the fat silhouette of Sergeant Hogg standing on it told us it was out of bounds. We cautiously stepped into the cold water. First it was ankle deep, then waist deep and soon we were up to our chests. It was hell trying to maintain my footing while the current buffeted me, I can honestly say that I feared for my life. It was freezing and there was every chance I would be swept off into a watery grave. That was it. Without further ado I retreated from that wet environment and returned to the bank. Drenched through I slopped my way to the bridge and I'd face the consequences when I got there. The consequences were an outraged Sergeant Hogg. "I can't do it." I told him. He told me I could and to prove his point he produced a sixteen foot branch out of nowhere and chased me off the bridge with it. With an awful feeling of impending doom I went back into the raging torrent. Sergeant Hogg was right, I did do it but I really thought I would perish that night. I was petrified.

Chapter 4   The Agony Piles On

We would return to Stanford again one day but, in the meantime, back in Bassingbourn nothing had changed. The NCOs still ran us ragged and the cockroaches still ran the cookhouse. There was still a lot to learn here and one of those things was drill. You were no good to the Army if you couldn't swing your arms and stay in step with your mates so they placed great importance on this particular skill. The RSM was a small, growling Royal Anglian whose name escapes me, but he would stand in front of the platoon and bark orders like an angry terrier. Nobody could understand a word he said but, like me, they just did what the bloke next to them did. If it was the right thing then all was well. If it wasn't, then the RSM would foam at the mouth and bark louder. Quite often he would march across our ragged line, constantly criticising our appearance. "Look at the state of you!" he would bellow, "You look like a bag of shit tied in the middle! What are you larfin' at?!" Then he would march away, ramrod straight with his pace stick tucked under his arm.

"WOT ARE YOU LARFIN AT?!"

It was he who taught us to salute, long way up, short way down. Up two three, down two three. Then we would march round the square in threes and salute him as we passed him. After about 2 hours of that he allowed us a NAAFI break. It came as a big surprise to me when I saw him one night as I walked to the NAAFI and I threw up a very smart salute. He went absolutely ape shit. I then learnt that you only salute commissioned officers. Oh well.

I can't remember the name of our platoon commander either, probably because we hardly ever saw him. He was a commissioned officer, a young Lieutenant. I remember that he joined us when it came to respirator training in the gas chamber; obviously it was an officer's perk to see the men die from CS gas. The gas chamber was a small brick building with a steel door; a door scarred by finger nails on the inside. One by one we filed into the chamber with our respirators firmly clamped on our faces. Inside there was a thin veil of grey smoke hanging in the air. This was CS gas and looked quite harmless at the moment, not very threatening at all. It couldn't have been too bad because our platoon commander stood in the middle without his respirator and he didn't seem to die. The steel door was closed and the Lieutenant called the first man forward inviting him to remove his respirator and recite his name, rank and number. The man duly obliged and when he got to the third digit of his number he promptly collapsed, choking to death. Suddenly that thin, grey veil that hung in the air took on a sinister presence. But there was worse to come. Freiberg was a likeable lad but he was cursed with a speech impediment. He stammered like nobody I'd ever known and it became worse when he panicked. He bravely stepped up to the officer, took a deep breath and removed his respirator. "T..t..two..f..f..four..." then lapsed into a coughing fit that would have killed a lesser mortal. The officer was quick to see the danger. "Sorry soldier, what was that again?" he asked. Needless to say more finger trails were added to the steel door that day. He was eventually released into the fresh air, eyes streaming and snot flowing freely. We learnt that there are people who are immune to the effects of CS gas. Such was the case with the platoon commander. Me? I just choke to death with the rest of them.

Back on the parade square RSM terrier taught us more drill movements. He told us that if you make a mistake - stand still. If you shuffled about you would attract attention to yourself and then incur the wrath of God. But if you stood still then you might just get away with it. I quickly found out that that this doesn't apply when you're facing the opposite way to everyone else. Meanwhile he still mocked our turnout. "There is shit on the end of my pace stick soldier!" he would bellow as he jabbed one of the lads with his pace stick. The standard reply would have been "Not on this end mate!" but none of us were that brave. There would be more trips to that hallowed ground before we could have our passing out parade.

More visits were made to the Barton Road ranges where we used our 'best friends' to throw lead at the fig. 11 targets. We weren't always on the firing line, sometimes a few of us would be detailed off as butt party. This is where you pushed the targets up so the others had something to fire at. This was usually an uneventful procedure and the only occasional excitement came when a round hit the embankment and threw dirt down your collar. So targets would go up and 7.62 rounds would zip over your head followed by the thump as it hit the sandbank. There was the odd ricochet but that didn't worry us too much. But when the General Purpose Machine Gun (GPMG) opened up you could see the tracer rounds flying about all over the place! Now it looked dodgy. Firing was cancelled for the rest of the week because the top brass discovered that the sandbank hadn't been cleared out for some time. But that was OK; we still had other weapons to be trained with...

The Carl Gustav 84mm anti-tank gun was a big beast and fired a fat tank busting shell. It looked like a big green drain pipe and we learnt in the classroom that there was no recoil because the shell came out of the front and the back blast shot out the rear. Now we were on the anti-tank range with this monster and our chance came to fire it. A two man team operated this gun: a No.1 to fire it and a No.2 to load it and check the back blast area. That was a very important part of firing this thing, checking that area behind us. Because if there was anyone standing there when you fired it they would be reduced to a pile of charred bones. I was the No.1 so I gave the order to load. The No.2 swung the venturi open, slammed in the shell and checked to the rear. "Loaded!" he yelled.

I put my eye to the rubber eyepiece of the sights and espied the rusty tank hull on the range. I deftly flicked the safety off and squeezed the trigger. There was a boom and the classroom theory was correct, there was no recoil. But the instructors omitted to mention the air displacement that hit you when the shell left the barrel. It felt like someone had smashed me in the nose with a sandbag full of concrete. I didn't even look to see if I'd hit the target I was still stunned by the shockwave. Then the NCO hit me on the helmet telling me to give the order to reload. Reload? Did I really want to fire another one?

Another range and another tube but this one was a lot smaller. It was the 2" mortar, a simple weapon where you slid the small shell into the tube and fired it by pulling the lanyard. The shell would pop out of the tube and make a graceful arc towards the target. What could possibly go wrong? I stood the mortar firmly on the ground, angled it and slid the shell down the tube. The target was a small copse about 100 metres away. I pulled the lanyard, the shell popped and I waited to spot the tell-tale trail of smoke heading for the target. "What are you looking for?" enquired the instructor. "The smoke trail Corporal!" I replied. "Really?" he said, "Try looking up there." I looked up and sure enough the 2" mortar shell was homesick and making its way back. It thumped into the ground about 10 feet in front of us and belched its smoke out. Lucky for us it wasn't high explosive. Simplicity itself eh?

Back on the 30 metre range where we were first introduced to our 'friends', we stood facing the targets with the sub machine-gun (SMG). This was a 9mm weapon used in close quarter battle and we had a full magazine to fire off. Unfortunately these would only be single shots and there was no blasting away on auto. The safety catch on this weapon operated in two stages, one click for those single shots, two clicks to send a stream of hot lead at the targets. So there was I, taking up the prone position under the watchful eye of Sergeant Hogg. "Three single shots in your own time go on!" he shouted. I took a firm grip of the weapon and eased the safety catch off. Now, was that one click or two? I squeezed the trigger and a string of rounds rattled out of the barrel. I guess it was two clicks then. Sergeant Hogg demonstrated his displeasure by banging on my helmet with a stick.

It was Sergeant Hogg that trained us in the gentle art of bayonet charging. In front of us stood a frame supporting a man shaped bunch of sandbags and we had our bayonets fixed. "When you charge the enemy," said our illustrious Sergeant, "I want you to scream at him!! I want you to scare him to death before you reach him with that dangerous bayonet!!" Without further ado the first man charged at the sandbags and poked it with his bayonet. After a couple of others went through Sergeant Hogg stopped the proceedings and gathered us together for a fatherly chat. "Fuckin' fairies," he said at length. He then decided that his fellow Geordie, Forsythe, was best suited to demonstrate the passion and the anger required. Forsythe stood on the start point and went for it. "DIE HOGG YOU FAT BASTARD!!" he screamed and thrust his bayonet into the sandbag, thrashing about like a pit bull terrier with PMT. Sergeant Hogg watched Forsythe return to the line, watching him with a very wary eye. "Next..." he said, still watching Forsythe.

Forsythe shows his prowess with a bayonet.

We'd been at Bassingbourn for some time now; our fitness was improving a little, while our bed boxes didn't. Mine was starting to look like a road accident. But the higher ups decided we could go out of camp for the night and paint the town red (or olive drab!) Some went into Royston, others went into Cambridge (Anabel's) while me and a few others stayed closer to home and went off to the Wagon and Horses pub. Wherever anyone went we all came back pissed as farts. This was a shame really because we had drill next morning. Because it was raining we were all marched into an empty hangar. At first everything went fairly reasonable but, after half an hour or so, the previous night's alcohol started to kick in. The first to waver was a bloke in the centre rank. He shuffled to the right then he shuffled to the left. He then wobbled back and wobbled forward. When he finished wobbling he fell flat on his face. Being highly trained soldiers and having a great sense of camaraderie we left him there. The instructor observed the soldier on the floor, approached in great strides and poked his head through the front rank. "Did this soldier have breakfast this morning!?" he yelled. Looking at the pasty faced body on the ground I think you could safely assume he did have breakfast. Two men were detailed to carry the body to one side so the rest of us could carry on marching. Before long, several other men collapsed with alcohol exhaustion and were carried off to join the first. Me, I just managed to stay upright and marched about in a coma.

We revisited Stanford to carry out escape and evasion exercises and night patrols. There was one river crossing but we did that in an assault boat so I was happy about that. On one patrol I was given the job of wireman and being a training area there should be lots of that I would have imagined. If we came across any wire obstacles I would have to crawl forward and breech it. When we came across the first batch of coiled barbed wire I was overjoyed. We all got down in the prone position and I made my way forward, clutching the wire cutters. It was a rusty old concertina barbed wire fence so it wouldn't be too difficult to snip through. Brandishing the cutters I set about the first snip and it cut easily. When I cut the last one the fence sprang apart and the still night air was suddenly filled with the racket of old compo tins rattling away! Being a concertina fence it was like a coiled spring and was filled with old tin cans. Apparently someone should have held the wire either side to stop it springing apart. Oh well, it certainly got the adrenalin going.

Another night and another patrol, but this time we were looking for the enemy. Our patrol of four men melted into the night and crept around looking for the foe, blank firing weapons at the ready. Being keen to let off a few blanks, my rifle was cocked and the safety catch was off. Probably not one of my better ideas. After a few hours of stumbling about in the dark and not finding anyone to shoot we made our way back. The return journey was much the same as the outbound one, all done very quietly and undetected. Maybe there was nobody else about. Maybe they were all tucked up in their green maggots. Then, suddenly, a loud bang shattered the silence causing everyone to jump. I jumped the highest; it was my weapon that had gone off! I must have been idly playing with the trigger and my 'friend' became over excited. I could hardly pretend it wasn't me; I was the only one standing in a cloud of cordite. This event was known as an accidental discharge, or AD. It was considered a very serious offence, for obvious reasons, and I should have been hung for it. But the Corporal escorting our patrol must have taken pity on me because when we returned to our camp he told the platoon commander that "Russell thought he saw something and took a shot at it." I was off the hook but I can promise you that I wouldn't be doing that again. Some years later it became known as a negligent discharge and the whole weight of the British Army would come down on you. Lesson learnt.

Chapter 5   Choppers and Battle Camp

At Bassingbourn we continued to run a lot and drill a lot but every morning started the same with banging of broom handles on bed frames. Once you got cleaned and dressed, the room inspection would commence. Sergeant Hogg and his Corporals would creep along each bed space, his beady little eyes scouring every detail. Every now and again he would poke his broom handle into a bed box and launch it across the room. Mine was a favourite. He also took a dislike to our best boots regardless of how shiny they were, he'd pick up a pair and a look of disgust would appear on his face. Then he'd march to the window and throw the offending footwear out into the morning air. By the time he finished the room looked worse than before we tidied it. He once inspected me and asked if I'd shaved that morning. I told him I had nothing to shave. But he convinced me that I should shave every morning with everyone else. I felt a bit of a fraud standing in the washroom 'shaving' my non-existent beard.

But the final exercise - battle camp - was fast approaching. This would take place in Warcop, Cumbria. Before we went off there though we had a spot of helicopter training, something I was very much looking forward to. We were marched out to the wasteland behind the barracks and lined up in 'sticks' and before long, huge Wessex helicopters appeared and landed. Prior to boarding the aircraft I couldn't help but notice the big exhausts, they looked like dustbins poking out of its body. You noticed them again when you clambered aboard because the heat and the fumes almost took your skin off. We all sat there with half a suntan each. That's OK though, we'll board from the other side next time and even the colour up. I thought it was marvellous being flown around in these wonderful flying machines, a real thrill. My love of helicopters still lives with me now.

Now it was time to depart for Warcop and our final battle camp. When we first came to Bassingbourn, Minden platoon was split into two because of the number of blokes on our intake, so we had Minden A and Minden B. As the training progressed some of the men fell to the wayside, either getting back squadded or simply leaving. This transition from Civvy to Soldier was no easy feat. The battle camp was the last obstacle before our passing out parade; fail this and you would go back four weeks and go through it all again. Whatever happened at Warcop, we all had to stick it out together and remain positive. When we arrived in Cumbria it was pissing down. I wouldn't have minded but the sun was starting to shine in Bassingbourn when we left. "If it ain't raining, it ain't training" said our wise old Sergeant Hogg. The sight of the camp in Warcop was depressing and made us yearn for the luxury of Bassingbourn. It was made up of ancient wooden huts furnished with old bedsteads and a potbellied stove. It looked like something out of The Great Escape... without the escape bit. This would be our home for the next week or so but we didn't have to worry about the poor accommodation because our instructors informed us that we would be spending most of our time out in the rain.

One of the tasks we had to complete was the thirty mile march. We would be dropped off in the middle of nowhere and march back to camp, with full kit and weapons. On the way back we would pop into the Tan Hill pub, Britain's highest pub, and we would partake of a pint. The lorry dropped us off and we began the long march back, hill after hill.

"Oh, the pub must be over the next hill then ..."

After an eternity, the Corporal informed us that the pub was just over the next hill. No it wasn't. Someone must have stolen it. "It must be the next one then," he said. We marched down that hill and up the next one. No pub. Were we on the right road? "Maybe the next one," the Corporal said. Several miles later we actually found the pub, it really did exist. Never was a pint so gratefully received.

Then we pressed on again. Along the way one of the lads was clearly struggling. Nobody wanted to see anyone back squadded at this stage so I carried his weapon, someone else took his webbing and two blokes half carried him. Between us we would ensure that we finished this together, that's the way of the Army. Back in Stalag Warcop a foot inspection was held. I had two so I passed. But it was blisters they were looking for, untreated they would cause further problems. My feet were fine but one bloke looked like his foot had activated its airbag.

Dawn attacks were a wonderful sight. With the platoon being split into two, we were often pitched against each other and these dawn attacks were no different. Our platoon was the first to attack their position. Just before first light we crept up on them, quietly and stealthily with surprise being our ally. The first flare went up and signalled the start of our attack and we went in with blanks blazing, more flares, para-flares, shamoolies and thunder flashes. It was a glorious sight, the Devil's own disco from hell. We were actually enjoying ourselves. Then me and my mate skirmished up to their machine gun trench where the GPMG was spitting its hail of death at us but we didn't waver. I knelt down and fired on the position which caused the gunner to duck into his trench. Then my mate ran over the trench pinching the gun as he went. I had to laugh when the gunner popped up clutching at thin air trying to grab the gimpy! My partner took advantage of this lapse and ran round firing both the gimpy and SLR from the hips. Very Audie Murphy. At the end of this frenzied assault we were both taken to one side and were told that pinching people's guns wasn't cricket. We thought it was a good idea at the time; anyway, the following morning they would have their revenge…

Next morning it was our platoon's turn to get an early morning call with the enemy rattling their blanks off and chucking thunder flashes around willy nilly. We were all stood to, defending our position from the advancing hordes. The first casualty was one of our lads who took cover in the sleeping bay of his trench. No sooner had he got in there than a thunder flash followed him in. Having clambered in there, it left nowhere else to go so he curled up in a ball as the pyrotechnic exploded. There was a blast of smoke and feathers from his sleeping bag and the blast split his boot open. War's a nasty business. Our second casualty was a lad still in his sleeping bag. The enemy swarmed through our defences and pinched his sleeping bag with him still in it. They quickly claimed he was a prisoner of war.

"Oy! A bit early for this malarkey aint it?!"

After the bloodshed we were well and truly battered and we had a man down. It later transpired that they had taken him back to their position and tied him to a tree where they tortured him mercilessly. Snowball was his chief tormentor. Snowball was a big black guy and was a patron of Anabel's nightclub in Cambridge. "When we get back to Bassingbourn," said Snowball, "we're off to Anabel's and you're paying for the taxi!" "Piss off!" replied the prisoner and got roughed up for his troubles. "And the taxi back!" said Snowball. Our hero told him to piss off again. More rough treatment ensued until our man grew weary. "Alright!" he said, "I'll pay for the taxi!" With that Snowball sauntered off. "But it'll have no fuckin' wheels on it!" shouted the captive in defiance. Again he got a beating. They eventually released him about 12 hours later, probably on the orders of an NCO who didn't fancy trawling through the next of kin forms.

We spent the next night in the comfort of Stalag Warcop preparing for the final battle run that would begin in the morning. It was only 23:00 hours and we were in desperate need of amusement. That's when we noticed Sheriff tucked up in his bed. He was always the first to get to bed because then he could be first in the breakfast queue at the cookhouse. He lived for his breakfast and would kill for a fry up. As soon as he nodded off we crept over and carefully adjusted his watch. We then clattered about in the room to give the impression we were getting up. Sheriff looked at his watch, got dressed then shot out of the door clutching his eating irons. The rest of us got into bed. Poor Sheriff was outside in the rain and probably cursing the duty cook for being late. He was still there when the camp guard came across him and told him what time it really was. Needless to say he wasn't a happy chappy when he got back to the room and found everyone curled up in their beds. If we weren't so knackered his grumbling stomach would have kept us awake all night.

Morning came and we were all rudely awakened by the NCOs. I think Sheriff squeezed past them to get to the cookhouse. After breakfast we gathered all our kit and weapons and were transported to the live firing range. Range? It was a huge swathe of countryside littered with figure 11 targets, trenches and other bits and pieces required for battle. It went on for miles. Our start point was a line of trenches, mine being full of water with a duckboard bobbing about in it. I couldn't see the point of starting the battle run soaked to the skin so I happily went prone alongside it. The gruff NCO put me right on that point and encouraged me to enter the trench. ("Get your fuckin' arse in there!!") I jumped in the hole, the duckboard sank and the water came past my knees. Sheriff did confirm that it had been raining the night before. Then the battle run began. With a full magazine of live rounds I started to pick off targets from my watery hole. Then we advanced forward, skirmishing up to our second firing point. Putting on a fresh mag I lined my sights up on the target to my front. I fired one shot and the plate came off the bottom of the magazine leaving the spring and a load of rounds lying around my elbows. Just what you don't need in the heat of battle! It's really difficult picking up rounds out of the grass when you have a Corporals boot up your arse and a big stick banging on your helmet. It could have been worse; it could have been the other way around. We all pushed on with us riflemen firing at the targets while Forsythe, with his gimpy, took out targets to the left and the right. That's when we all noticed the lone sheep on the horizon, as did Forsythe. You could see the bullet hits from his gun chewing up the ground, winding their way to the sheep then it suddenly disappeared. "I saw that Forsythe!" bellowed Sergeant Hogg. Twenty minutes into the battle we passed the steaming carcass on our route, its woolly legs pointing skyward. But there was no time for lamb chops, we had to move on. At the end of it we were all wet, covered in mud and totally knackered. But we made it and we all passed.

A few days later we returned to Bassingbourn, a world of comfy beds, clean sheets and lots of drill. Yes, we continued to bash that square in preparation for the passing out parade and the RSM was on fine form. "What do you look like!!? When you were born your mother must have thrown away the baby and kept the afterbirth!! What are you larfin' at!!?" We also did a bit of urban warfare because there was a bit of a problem in Northern Ireland. What was all that about then? You didn't see that on the posters. Apparently the current troubles flared up in 1969 but we were told not to worry about it because it would probably be over quicker than it started... Before the long awaited parade we were to be badged. So where was I going? The Corporal from the Queen's Regiment asked me the same question. "Queen's? Anglians? Fusiliers?" he asked. I had no idea and told him so. "Queen's it is then!" he said passing me my badge, collar dogs and buttons. Being from Coventry I should have been in the Fusiliers but I knew nothing about county regiments and such like, and that's how I ended up serving in a southern outfit. With buttons sewn onto our No2s and collar dogs and badges in place we went on to the parade square. The RSM behaved himself and appeared respectful of us but that was probably more to do with the turnout of parents rather than us. The parade went off without incident and we could now call ourselves soldiers. We had very little time to reflect on the last three months because we had to vacate our rooms for the next intake. We said our farewells and headed off in different directions to join our units. I, John Curry, Dave Marshall, Snowball and a few others went off to The 3rd Battalion The Queen's Regiment in Tidworth, Salisbury Plain.

Chapter 6   Otterburn and Motorman

May 1972

I enjoyed Tidworth. For the few of us that went to the 3rd Battalion we had the pleasure of being in the hands of seasoned veterans, some of the older ones had served in Aden but all of them had just returned from 2 years in Ballykinler in Northern Ireland. I joined 4 platoon, B Company at Lucknow Barracks and the first thing they told me was that the Battalion was off to Otterburn the following week. Fancy that, I've only been here 5 minutes and I'm going to Norway already! No I wasn't, Otterburn is in Northumberland near the Scottish border. But the disappointment soon dissipated when they explained that it was for helicopter training so that we could fulfil our air portable role. Lucky old me. So I spent the following week getting to know my new mates. The section commander was Corporal 'Chalky' White and his 2ic was Lance Corporal Bill Kempton. The section was Trevor Francis, Bob Tufnell, John Docherty, Steve Terry and Chris Gherratty. They were all decent blokes and took the time to introduce me to members of the other sections within the platoon. They also introduced me to The Drummer Boy pub on the Tidworth high street but that goes without saying.

June 1972

After a week off socialising, the whole battalion was packed onto a troop train and headed north. It seemed to take years to get to Otterburn but we did get there and there were more than enough helicopters to keep me happy. It was also wonderful weather; the Quarter Master must have forgotten to order the rain! Basically we got picked up by helicopter, flew to another grid reference, alighted the aircraft and then we would do some soldier like marching to our next pick up point. All this in glorious sunshine, what a way to earn a living. The marching was littered with occasional section attacks using blanks and these were overseen by marshals. At one point we were ambushed by another platoon but we felt we had blasted our way out of it honourably. The marshal said we had all been killed. "Just a flesh wound!" we shouted as we ran off through the woods. On another march we had a river crossing but, unlike Stanford, this was daytime in the sun and the river was calm and only knee deep. We crossed it easily except the 84mm anti-tank gun man dropped his weapon when he stumbled. So we all thrashed about in the water until we found it. The whole point of the exercise was to practise the various ways to disembark from the helicopters and one method was to jump off when the flying machine came into the hover. There were two lights on board to assist us, red for ready and a green one to go. There was also the loadmaster to ensure things went right. The helicopter flew us around the Northumberland countryside and as it approached the landing zone the red light illuminated. The loadmaster, who sat in the doorway judging the distance to the ground, was most surprised when one of our soldiers shot past him and went treading air in the attempt to defy gravity. Luckily his legs broke his fall. Hell of a way to get off an exercise. It was one of those 'leap off' episodes when I encountered a problem. I was the last one off while the helicopter hovered but the strap of my large pack caught up in the machine's airframe. Obviously the helicopter was on a tight schedule and immediately began its accent, which left me in a dilemma. I could hang on to my worldly goods and go off like Mary Poppins or I could let go. I decided on the latter and watched the helicopter and my large pack

"Where's Russell got to?"

disappear into a tiny dot. Next day, I'm glad to say, I was reunited with my luggage.

Between marching and flying there was a lot of waiting, a case of 'hurry up and wait'. Some of the men would get their heads down while others cleaned their weapons or chatted. The devil makes work for idle hands and we soldiers were no different than anyone else. Bearing that in mind my mate broke open some blanks while I stripped a length of porcupine grass. We placed the liberated powder onto a large pack which one of the sleepers was using as a pillow. Then I took a piece of the stripped porcupine grass, carefully poked it into the powder and lit the end of it. We both sat back and relaxed as the grass slowly smouldered. Suddenly our sleeping friend was awoken by the flash of the powder and the smell of singed hair. The things you do when you're bored.

After 2 weeks of the flying circus we were all called into the camp theatre where the CO wanted to address the Battalion. He informed us that, due to problems in Northern Ireland, the helicopter training was to be cut short. Apparently no-go areas had sprung up all over the place and we would be heading off to Londonderry as part of Operation Motorman. So we all travelled back to Tidworth then had a few weeks leave. The Army were good like that, if they sent you some place where you could get killed they gave you leave so you could say goodbye to family and friends. I did go on leave and, at the end of it, I said my goodbyes. My mum gave me a big hug and dad shook my hand. "Good luck son," he said and really meant it. I then departed to the old fire station in Coventry and caught the coach back to Tidworth, sleeping off the beer as I went.

July 1972

Back at Tidworth we made preparations for the emergency tour of Londonderry. One task we were expected to carry out was the snatch squad, a technique used during a riot to haul out the ringleaders. So all the platoons mustered on the football pitch and we were split into 2 groups; one of the groups would riot while the other would go in, grab someone in a gooseneck hold and drag him back. I was with the first group that rioted and I wasn't too pleased to see Bob Tapper making a bee line for me. Bob was L/Cpl Tapper, a Fijian who was well over six foot and was all solid muscle. He got hold of me and dragged me back to the line like he was towing a dead sock behind him. Now we had to dive into the rioters so we rushed in and it came as no surprise that nobody wanted to tackle big Bob. That's OK; I went in and refused to be intimidated by him. Bob, being a gentleman, held out his hand and allowed me to place a hold on him. I proudly took him back to the line with him squealing all of the way. All faked of course.

After packing our weapons and equipment we went to Liverpool docks and boarded the Sir Galahad, a flat bottomed LSL, which would transport us across the Irish Sea to Belfast. I'd be telling a lie if I said I wasn't worried, because I was. But I consoled myself with the thought that I was in the hands of veterans who had just spent 2 years in the province. The ship wasn't exactly a cruise liner, more like a tramp steamer. On the deck were numerous portakabins and below it was full of Chinese crew. There were no cabins for us passengers so we just lay down where we could with me in the hold sprawling over large packs and kit bags. We travelled through the night and in the morning the iconic Harland and Wolfe cranes could be seen looming into view. Once we disembarked we were loaded onto trucks and driven out through the gates where the 'reception committee' greeted us with a bombardment of bricks and bottles, with some of the missiles finding their through the canvas flaps. How lovely of them to make the effort so early in the morning. The wagons rolled out of Belfast and made their way to Londonderry where we passed through the Creggan and arrived at Piggery Ridge. Well, what a surprise. We clambered out of the trucks and we were amazed to be confronted by a cook slaving over his No.1 burner surrounded by barbed wire. Was that it? Where were the barrack rooms and bullet proof walls? The question of barrack rooms was soon answered when the portakabins arrived, the same ones that were on the LSL. It suddenly dawned on me that there was a lot of work to be done here. And I wasn't wrong. Our emergency tour at Piggery Ridge turned out to be one of the most gruelling tours of my career. If you weren't patrolling the streets you would be on guard duty, and if you weren't on guard you were filling and carrying thousands of sandbags. If you weren't doing any of those things then you would be providing protection for the Royal Engineers as they laid the infrastructure for the new born camp. And for those of you who thought spud bashing died out with National Service I can assure you it was alive and well and thrived at Piggery Ridge. Sleep? It felt like a luxury that didn't exist in this part of the world.

1972 in Northern Ireland would turn out to be the bloodiest year for the British Army but, even so, there was still much humour amongst the ranks. Like the night I stood in a sanger, a sandbag pill box mounted on scaffolding, armed with my trusty SLR and a night scope. It looked over the back of the houses of the Creggan Estate so we could spot any sneaky people creeping up on our position. As I stood there I was suddenly aware of the thunderous sound of many pounding feet. "Shit," I thought, "the whole of the estate is descending onto my sanger!" I quickly flicked the toggle switch on the night scope and placed it to my eye. As the circuitry buzzed in my ear I saw it, loads of them. Nobody told me there were horses in the field below, all of them happily stampeding past my post.

The street patrols weren't as bad as I had imagined, it was a bit like patrolling through the streets of Coventry except you were wearing a uniform carrying a rifle and everyone was hostile. Whenever we took any verbal off the locals I never took it personally, the uniform was the 'wanker' not me, surely? I remember one particular young lady who we passed most days, very pretty with a shy smile. I grew quite fond of her in a funny sort of way so I thought I would give her a kindly greeting next time I saw her. Sure enough we passed her again one day. "Good morning," I said cheerily. "Fuck off British bastard!" she replied and spat at me. What a shame, she really was pretty.

Someone not so pretty was a hard faced housewife who never did see eye to eye with us and you wouldn't want to tackle her in a wrestling match. We met her walking down the street while on patrol. "Feck off home ye British bastards!" she screamed, "You don't belong here!!" It just so happened that John Docherty was leading the patrol who was born and bred in Northern Ireland. "But I am home," he said in his unmistakable accent. The poor woman nearly had a fit. She was stuck for words for at least 2 seconds. "You.. you feckin' traitor!!" she bellowed. And that's all you could hear as we continued our happy little patrol.

Operation Motorman did have a serious purpose. We were here to clear the no-go areas. The locals had sealed off areas by putting up barricades of burnt out vehicles, barbed wire and other rubbish and it was about to come to an end. Sergeant Joe Kaye-Lesser (affectionately known as K-L or Big Joe) was our platoon Sergeant and he gathered us together in the early hours of the morning and told us that Motorman was about to begin. The engineers would clear the bigger obstacles with their Scooby Doo vehicles and we would deal with the smaller things like the barbed wire. "If anything will stop a Saracen its barbed wire," he told us. "It punctures the tyres." Joe often amazed us with his broad knowledge. He decided the best way to remove the wire was to reverse the Saracen up to it and drag it away with a piece of rope and a grappling hook. Off we went, under the cover of darkness, and found our first entanglement of wire. The vehicle quickly reversed up to it and Joe leapt off with the grappling iron. He threw it in there, leapt back onto the vehicle shouting "Go!" The driver put his foot down and we went down the road with a shower of sparks in our wake. We dumped that onto some waste ground and went in search of more. We reversed up to a second pile of wire and Joe jumped out and did his thing. "Go!" he shouted as he stepped aboard. But Joe wasn't as quick as he thought and he underestimated the reflexes of the driver. The Saracen roared off with Joe's foot still in the wire. We all looked on in amazement at Joe's boot and its shower of sparks trailing behind our wagon. Laugh? We nearly told the driver to stop...

Later that day we were on a routine patrol in the same vehicle when Joe spotted one of his old buddies from a neighbouring battalion near The Raith. The Raith was a roundabout on the edge of our patrol area. He ordered some of us off and to take up all round defence while he had a chat with his mate. I decided to use the vehicle for cover and rested my elbows on the body work, weapon poised and looking mean. When I saw three young lads heading in our direction I went into looking mega-mean. Just as they passed behind about three zillion volts zapped through me. My body took on the properties of a bin liner. Luckily my rifle was attached to my wrist with the sling so I managed to keep hold of that. Did these three lads have some sort of secret weapon? Did they possess super-human powers? I went to the rear of the vehicle to seek advice and I found the occupants laughing their heads off. Apparently there is a generator on board and, when it's switched on, it electrifies the outer skin of the Saracen. When they saw me leaning on the wing they had switched it on. They did inform me that if it was wet it would have blown me across the road. That's OK, I can take a joke. Bastards. Then Joe K-L came striding back ordering us onto the vehicle. We thought this would be hilarious so we flicked the generator on and awaited his boarding. "What's that buzzing noise?" he asked while standing a few inches from the armoured body. We managed to convince him that it was the air conditioning. Joe shrugged and hopped onto the vehicle. Rats! He hadn't made an earth. Then they told him about me and he pissed himself.

One night we were on foot patrol doing the usual things to stay alive. Things like avoiding the pools of light from lampposts, steering clear of white painted walls and keeping on the move. It was a residential area so we went close to the houses which meant walking through gardens and 'hedge-hopping'. We found the best way to get over a hedge was to lean into it, swing your legs over and continue on. We got very good at that, it became a nice, smooth flowing movement. We were doing this that night when Steve Terry was our tail end Charlie. We all passed over one particularly flimsy hedge with ease until Steve got there. He leaned into the hedge, swung his legs over and the whole fragile foliage flattened leaving Steve like a turtle on its back. We picked him up out of the twigs and carried on. As far as Steve was concerned the bushier the bush the better.

On another night patrol we were going about minding our own business when we got a contact report over the radio. One of our patrols had been fired on and the radio operator had been hit. We all ran towards the Swilley Gardens area and found the radio operator, Jim Hedges, lying in the gutter. Luckily Jim hadn't been hit but the Armalite round caught him in the radio harness and spun him around like a top. Jim was uninjured but he was most upset that the sniper picked on him. According to another radio transmission the round had come from one area, shot down the road and took a sharp left at the traffic lights. I think he got confused in all the excitement. Back at Piggery Ridge Charlie Williamson and I found a rare moment of respite so I strolled off to the NAAFI tent and got two cups of tea. The trip to the tent was uneventful and I had a rather pleasant chat to the corporal running it. Then I picked up the two plastic cups and steadily made my way back, being awfully careful not to spill the contents. Just as I passed between two of the portakabins a shot rang out and I was showered with shit from the roof. Sensing the danger I quickened my step. Then a second shot rang out followed by more roofing flying through the air! That was it - I was off! I managed to get to my own portakabin with two empty cups and a pair of blistered hands. It was clear to me that an enterprising IRA sniper was trying to pick off the tea boy before we could build our sandbag wall. But that wasn't the case at all. It turned out that someone from another platoon had just come off patrol and was clearing his weapon in his cabin when he accidentally let a round off through the ceiling. In his panic he let rip with another. The Army frowned on this kind of thing, especially with live rounds, so the soldier concerned was locked away for some time. Which just goes to show, scaring the living shit out of the tea boy is a sin.

Picking off the teaboy is a sin!

John Docherty had a knack for putting the wind up people. He was a keen darts player and everywhere John went, his dart board went too. After coming off a patrol he decided to practise with his arrows but then he was distracted by someone dropping an aerosol can on the floor. In one swift move he turned, threw his dart and pierced the can dead in the centre. If it wasn't bad enough having a punctured aerosol can spin around the room John went and ignited it with a flick of his lighter. It's amazing how quickly a dozen soldiers could vacate a portakabin. It was like soldiering with the Marx Brothers. As soon as the blazing missile got extinguished we all climbed into our sleeping bags for a few hours kip. Because, in the morning, we would have to go out in the early hours to monitor a protest march over internment...

Chapter 7   Internment and Dishwater

Internment was introduced in Northern Ireland the previous year and was designed to keep known bad people off the streets. Obviously the locals didn't think much of this idea and, on the first anniversary of its introduction, they were expected to pour onto the streets and voice their displeasure. In the early hours of the morning we marched down to the Creggan and took up our positions to oversee the march. At first it was very dark and very quiet, not a soul in sight and not a sound to be heard. Then, at about 04:00 hrs, the silence was broken by the sound of a solitary dustbin lid being banged on the ground some distance away. We all stood by our Saracen listening to this when a few more joined in. The dawn chorus Creggan style? Soon there was a whole orchestra of them. The sound grew closer and became louder and more frantic. We heard one dustbin lid growing weary. "Probably been wankin' all night," said someone from under his helmet. Soon they were upon us, hundreds of them banging and chanting. We all stood fast in our ponchos and helmets, rifles at the ready. As they all filed past it took a turn for the worse and bricks and bottles rained down on us with the small corner of a paving slab just missing me and bouncing off the Saracen. Marcus Welsby was one of our Lance Corporals and he caught a milk bottle full of white paint. It actually smashed on the vehicle but Marcus got the contents. We all gathered at the back of the wagon and reached in for the riot shields that lay there. "What are you doing with those?" It was the voice of our Captain speaking from the safety of the cupola. He was probably there to prevent any sneaky Irishmen from sneaking in. We explained to him about the rocks, bottles and the paint job that Marcus got. "Leave the shields where they are!" he said, "Otherwise you'll antagonise them!" Well, we wouldn't want to do that would we? By mid-morning it was all a distant memory and we headed back to Piggery Ridge to fill some more sandbags. Well it certainly made a change from dreaming about them...

Late that afternoon we were back on the street, on foot patrol, where we found the locals were very irritable. Maybe it was lack of sleep. After all they'd been awake since 4 o'clock. At one point the patrol paused and we took cover with one of the lads taking refuge in a front garden. Not a bad bit of cover but the woman of the house noticed him there and came stomping out. She was a big woman with no teeth, a head full of curlers and jowls like Roy Rogers' saddlebags. Not only wasn't she looking her best but she was in a bad mood too. "Ye British bastard ye!" she yelled, "Get your feckin' arse out of my feckin' garden!!" She continued with her barrage of abuse but the soldier stayed rooted to the spot. She was clearly unimpressed with this show of defiance and she told him so. Big Joe K-L saw the commotion and stepped over to reason with the woman but she just grew angrier. "Right yer Feckers!" she finally said, "I'm comin' back with a bowl of dishwater and if yer still there yer feckin getting it!!" She then stomped back into the house and returned with the promised bowl of slop. Joe moved between her and the soldier, continuing to reason with her. He then decided to bring an end to the conversation and tipped the bowl towards her, its contents cascading down her pinny. To say that she wasn't happy about that would be an understatement so we all made a tactical withdrawal. Soon we joined our Saracen, it was safer in there.

"OK lads, retreat to the wagon!"

Big Joe sat in the commander's cupola and I was at the back monitoring the headphones when the OC came on the air waves calling Joe's call sign. The conversation went something like: OC: "I've had a complaint from one of the locals." K-L: "Really Sir? Who was that?" OC: "Some woman reckons you assaulted her." K-L: "Sorry Sir, I didn't catch that." OC: "A woman says that she was drenched by British soldiers." K-L: "Sorry Sir, I must be in a dead spot. I can hardly read you." OC: "I said... oh sod it! I'll see you when you get back." Couldn't hear him? Tosh! He was as clear as a bell; Joe was just buying himself some thinking time. Joe K-L was my hero.

My baptism of fire in Northern Ireland was drawing to a close. The Coldstream Guards had arrived to take over and we sat on a truck waiting for our sniper patrol to return. When they did, we would all be transported to Belfast docks and board the LSL. We were still in the truck when a shot rang out. A sergeant in the Coldstream Guards had been shot and killed. Our sniper patrol returned fire but were unable to confirm a hit. The soldier returning fire was a young Indian lad, Private Bhatta. So it was with a tinge of sadness that we left Piggery Ridge. Just a quick note, when the sandbag wall was completed it appeared in the Guinness book of records as the biggest ever built and was credited to the Coldstream Guards. Just to put the record straight, we built most of that!

Chapter 8   Cyprus

Once we all got back to Tidworth we went on leave for a few weeks. Having dispensed with the flak jacket and combats I felt ten stone lighter. I spent most of the time having a drink with friends and family, shared some 'war stories' with my dad then caught the coach at the old fire station, sleeping all the way back to Tidworth as usual. Nothing had changed at Lucknow Barracks. I got back at 4 in the morning and just wanted to get my things put away into my locker and grab a few hours in bed. It was then I noticed the padlock securing my locker was on back to front. Who's been in here then? I opened it up and was confronted by a mess; someone had turned my locker upside down. As I climbed into bed I could hear the other lads chuckling under their sheets. The sods were always up to something. I once came off weekend leave and they had pulled all the springs from under my mattress and replaced them with flimsy string. I thought my bed had swallowed me.

To maintain fitness and enjoy ourselves it was decided that football would be good. It may well have been but they put me in goal. At the point where the opposing team were 15 up they charged my poorly defended goal yet again. Luckily the ball went over the bar, across the road and into the MT yard. "What a stroke of luck!" I thought as I ran across the road to ask the MT Sergeant for my ball back. When I returned to the pitch both teams were formed in a huddle. I had no idea what they were plotting but I kicked the ball into the small crowd. Being rubbish the ball missed them by two bus lengths so I ran across to see what the fuss was all about. Bhatta was lying on the floor turning blue and Chris Gherratty was attempting to resuscitate him. I dashed back to the MT yard and got the Sergeant to call an ambulance. The Land Rover ambulance arrived in minutes and Bhatta was stretchered on board. It then sped off with blue lights flashing and sirens wailing while the players complained because the game was held up. From then on my goal was better defended thanks to the deep ruts left by the Land Rover. We still lost. It was only when we got back to the room that we heard the news that Bhatta had died on the way to the hospital. He had choked and the crew were unable to save him despite their best efforts. Soon after that we found out that Bhatta did indeed hit the sniper in Londonderry, but he would never have known that. I still feel ashamed that I hadn't even learnt his first name.

At last, the Army were going to let me see the world just as they promised in those posters. We boarded our RAF VC10 at Brize Norton and within several hours we landed in Akrotiri in Cyprus. It was the early hours of the morning so, as the aircraft taxied, I put on my combat jacket and buttoned up. When the doors opened I stepped into the air. Phwoar, but it was hot. I unbuttoned my jacket, took it off and rolled up my shirt sleeves. Not only was it warm but there were palm trees too! There's a lot to be said for these foreign parts. We left the airfield in our buses which, no doubt, were whisking us off to our first class luxury accommodation. Actually our Company were dropped off at a dusty run-down camp near an old fishing village. Welcome to Zyyi. Later that morning we were formed up outside the stores collecting our blue berets, brassards, blue cravats and UN badges. Yes, we would be UN peacekeepers for the next six months in UNFICYP, an awesome responsibility.

Russell the U.N. peacekeeper, Cyprus

It would appear that the Greeks and the Turks weren't getting on especially well with each other so the UN were there to stop them fighting among themselves. Our Company Sergeant Major, Alan Prince, left us in no doubt how we would achieve this: drill, lots of it. We would spend most of our daylight hours marching up and down in the Zyyi dust while someone banged out the time on a dustbin with a stick. He made it perfectly clear that if we didn't get it right we would continue marching until a trench appeared beneath our boots.

I found Bill Kempton and Andy Hawker were a wonderful source of entertainment. Bill could often be heard strumming away on his guitar while sat on his veranda. Andy was a Brummy and it wasn't unusual to see him walking his lizard on a lead. (Jack Sear was someone else who would take his lizard on a walk with his lead except he didn't actually have a lizard on it. At first we thought he was working his ticket but it quickly transpired that he was just mad.) One day, Bill was gently strumming his guitar when Andy happened to pass by with his lizard. Andy thought it would be polite to introduce his lizard to Bill so he took it over and did just that. The lizard swivelled a beady eye at Bill then shot up his leg. Bill leapt onto his chair looking very much like the maid out of Tom and Jerry telling Andy to sod off with his lizard. Andy loved his lizard. Bill hated it.

I was on camp guard with Andy one night and my stag followed his. I wasn't surprised to see he had scrawled graffiti on the sentry box wall which read "Russell must not play night bombers on the shithouse". I knew there would be repercussions and they came in the shape of Provost Corporal White. Chalky to his mates but he didn't seem to have many of those. He hauled me into the guard room the next day and threatened to do unpleasant things to me if I didn't paint his sentry box and obliterate the offending scrawl. I felt a great sense of injustice so I told him Andy Hawker had done it. Corporal White thought that was very good of me, now he had two soldiers to paint his box. With a bucket of white paint in one hand and a brush in the other we began redecorating the Corporal's beloved sentry box. It only took about an hour so we reported back to Corporal White and he went to inspect our work. It turns out that he was very pleased with the job. Then he looked at his guardroom and decided the rocks bordering the garden would look nice if they were painted white too. (I say garden, it was merely a patch of dirt.) After about 20 rocks Andy hatched a plan. If we tipped the paint away into a nearby ditch we wouldn't be able to paint the rest. So that's what we did, then reported to the Corporal telling him we had run out of paint. "We've got no more paint left Corporal," we told him as he sat at his desk. "That's OK," he replied without looking up from his girlie mag, "Nip over to the stores and get another tin." We went to the stores and found the shelves full of white paint! I think Corporal White may have over ordered. We finished his rocks just after lunchtime and he let us off the hook. It turned out that Corporal 'Chalky' White wasn't such a bad bloke after all. Because one night Andy and myself were returning to camp after a few beers when we bumped into the Corporal. We braced ourselves for an ear-bending but no, instead he invited us to his bunk at the rear of the gatehouse and offered us a beer. Was it a trap that me and Andy had foolishly walked into? No it wasn't. The three of us had a great chat and it would appear that Chalky was somewhat of a loner in Zyyi because the rest of his provost mates were spread across Cyprus. He had been so bored that he painted a mural round his room, all in black silhouette depicting life from birth to the grave. A strange but likeable bloke.

Our own Corporal White was still with our platoon. He and John Docherty staggered into the room one night, both pissed and both intent on entertaining the troops. John attempted some baton twirling with a few fluorescent light tubes but, having smashed half a dozen of them, he gave up. Corporal White then took to the floor and told us about pain being all in the mind. To demonstrate this he smashed a beer bottle and appeared to drag it down his forearm. Then his forearm appeared to bleed! Was it a clever trick? No, he actually slashed his own arm! After that we all considered that he was a little nuts and gave him a wide berth…

Sergeant Major Prince still had us drilling up and down in the dust hoping to turn us into a smart rabble. He was a hard task master but in the evening he would mellow with a few brandy sours and join us in the camp bar. The bar was 'Dirty Dicks' run by Corporal Dick Leathers and, because we were out of sight of the locals, all sorts went on there. Somebody would climb onto a table to a rousing chorus of Zulu Warrior and a rolled up newspaper was inserted in an appropriate place. That would be fine in the UK but Cypriot paper was more like tissue and burns a lot quicker. There was a blinding flash followed by the waft of a singed arse. I'm glad to report that the participant survived his ordeal. When the Sergeant Major came in there was a limbo dancing competition taking place and he very much wanted to be a part of it. Who were we to argue? The broom handle was held at a reasonable height and the Sergeant Major readied himself. I offered to hold his brandy sour but he trusted no one where his drink was concerned. So there he was, knees bent, leaning back and his glass in his hand. He slowly edged forward under the broom handle. Then he fell flat on his back and the glass shattered. Blood and brandy sour went all over the floor and the only person not concerned about the carnage was the Sergeant Major himself. He thought it was a lot of fuss about nothing. It took a while before we eventually convinced him to attend the medical centre where they strapped his wrist up. Next morning he still had us marching up and down, barking out his orders and sporting a new crepe sweat band.

Now and again we would break free from the camp and taste the delights of Cyprus. (We found the women delightful! OK it cost a few bob but we were young lads and our loins would occasionally stir.) John Curry was still with us and his loins were in a constant state of stir. I never knew anyone like him, he was rampant. He could sniff out a brothel in a five mile radius, and if there wasn't one he'd build one. Then there was Phil Bradley, a really nice bloke who sported a rather grand handlebar moustache and false teeth. You knew when Phil had been out on the town because next morning he'd have no teeth. He had a habit of throwing up out of the taxi window on the return journey and his dentures would escape into the night air. The Cypriot countryside must have been littered with his dentures. I met Phil many years later at a reunion and have to report that he doesn't drink anymore. I would imagine the dental bills would have bankrupted him. But he's still a lovely bloke.

Dirty Dicks bar on the camp wasn't always a den for hardened drinkers; you could pop in during the day and partake of something non-alcoholic, like lemon tea. I often went in and found Dick Leathers a genial host. He always fascinated me with his knowledge and inventiveness. He would easily knock up all sorts of gadgets and gladly show everyone how they worked. He was quite amazing. But it was a night time when I was in there and met the entertainment committee who were scouting for talent. Christmas would soon be upon us and they needed soldiers to amuse the troops at the Christmas show. "Not me Buster," I told them "What could I possibly do on a stage?" "But you draw cartoons!" they said. That was true but how boring would that be on a stage? "But surely you could make people laugh," they insisted. Probably, if I fell over my boot laces and fell off the stage. No, I told them I would be no part of it; I'd rather be entertained by the other victims who were coerced into this madness.

Wonky Hibbert was another Brummy in our ranks. I met up with him in Limassol one night and we both ended up with the same loose woman. (Not at the same time I hasten to add!) It was probably a week or so later when Wonky passed me coming back from the toilet. "Fuckin' shite mate!" he said, "I've just been for a piss and it was like pissin' razor blades!" I nearly fainted! It could only mean one thing - the dreaded clap! The following morning I was first in the queue outside the pox doctor's office. The MO was Captain Fitzgerald, a likeable Irishman who was more than sympathetic regarding my dilemma. "If you haven't shown any symptoms," he said, "then I don't think you have anything to worry about." Then he kicked me in the leg. "Next time you have a screw wear a washer!" he said and sent me for a blood test to be on the safe side. That's where I met L/Cpl Scouse Gidman, our RAMC man. Having rolled up my sleeve he went straight in with the needle. I felt a pinch as it went in, followed by another. Scouse pulled on the plunger of the hypodermic and it filled with frothy pink blood. "Oops! Too far," said the manic medic. Cheers mate, I'll remember you. I passed this snippet of information on to Wonky and he burst out laughing. He never had any symptoms at all; he was just winding me up. What a shit...

We were still in Zyyi when Christmas arrived, my first Christmas from home and certainly the warmest one I had ever experienced. The day started with Officers and SNCOs waking you up with an urn of gunfire which was a cocktail of Army tea and industrial strength rum. You didn't drink it - you chewed it. Then you would walk out onto the veranda where the sun beat down on men who lay with fire buckets full of ice to keep the beer and Keo brandy cool. Oh well, in for a penny in for a pound. We all sweated over Christmas dinner in the cookhouse where we reckoned the turkey died of sunstroke. It was over this period that the 'entertainment committee' staged their grand Christmas show, musicians, comedians, sketches and... me. "But..!" I hear you cry, "You said you would be no part of it!" You're absolutely right, but in the interim period they had approached me again, and they caught me at a weak moment - I was pissed. Not only that but they also threw in a crate of beer. How could I say no? It sounded like a good deal with my beer goggles on. So there I was, in front of the troops, dressed up in drag. I don't know where they got the dress from but it fitted OK. (They didn't get it from Bassingbourn stores then!) I can't remember exactly how I started my routine; in fact I only remember two highlights.

"Don't even think it buster!"

The first was when I 'yoo-hoo'd' the OC of B Company, Major Gordon Crumley. "Wonderful night last night Gordon," I said. Then I dipped into my carrier bag and pulled out a pair of Y-fronts. "You left these at my flat last night, you naughty boy!" Even as I said it I couldn't believe I was saying it. Major Crumley sat on the hot plate at the back of the cookhouse and the look on his face said "You're a dead man Russell." The next bit I remember was at the end, Sergeant Brett was at the front and he took an unhealthy fancy to my legs. He leapt onto the stage but I found I could run quicker with my dress hitched up than he could with his trousers around his ankles. My honour was preserved. Andy Hawker got up there too, playing a raging poofdah singing material from Rambling Syd Rumpo. He was accompanied by Bill Kempton on his guitar. Bill didn't mind playing along but he looked a bit concerned when Andy ran his fingers through his thinning hair. At least Andy's lizard was nowhere in sight so he was glad about that.

After two months at Zyyi the companies rotated and we went to Kophinou although most of my time would be spent at Cliff OP, a small outpost on top of a hill. This was a sparse camp comprising 2 Nissan huts (one the kitchen, the other the accommodation), a lookout post, a kerosene powered shower and a thunderbox. As I recall there was Corporal Ken Arey, Ben Cartwright, John Curry, Ginger Johnson and myself. Ben Cartwright never ceased to amaze me with his cigarette rolling skills. He could sit there and roll a cigarette, nay, a perfect cigarette, with one hand. I was so impressed he tried to teach me this skill, bearing in mind I couldn't roll a fag with two hands! I watched with great attentiveness as he performed this amazing operation. However, when I attempted it, I just ended up with a pile of tobacco on the floor and a crumpled cigarette paper flapping in the breeze. But he did show me the art of how to strike a match with one hand. This was achieved by holding the box in the palm of your hand with the match poised over the striker. A deft flick of the fingers and the lit match appeared magically. I felt sure that impressive trick would come in handy one day.

The sentry box at Cliff OP was a strange setup. In the day it served its purpose well but at night the whole world needed to see that it was manned so we had to have a hurricane lamp in there. Yes, the world could see we were there but we couldn't see a thing out of it! There wasn't much to look at anyway. But I was in there one night, hopefully with the world watching, when a stone hit the window. I stood there wondering who would be throwing stones at my position when another one struck. I quickly leapt out and scoured the area but there wasn't a soul to be seen in the darkness. Back in the box another missile hit my window. I leapt out with my trusty SLR in one hand and the hurricane lamp in the other. "Funny buggers!" I called, expecting the lads to pop up from behind a rock. But they didn't. Then I looked at the base of my sentry box and saw dozens of May bugs shimmying about on their backs. At least they were taking notice of the light in my box. So I resumed my guard duty accompanied by the plinking of May bugs off the glass.

As far as thunderboxes go, this one was fairly comfortable although I wouldn't have fancied long periods sitting on it. Especially after I heard the story of another one at one of the other company locations. Apparently someone caught a wild cat and threw it in there. Obviously there was no escape for the feral feline until someone lifted the lid and sat on it whereupon the cat made a bid for freedom and clawed the unsuspecting soldiers arse. But this one was fine. It could have done with a lick of paint and some wallpaper perhaps but by and large it was OK. My only problem with it was after dark. You'd be sitting there doing your thing when the local Minaret (wailing tower) started calling everyone to prayer. What an awful sound that was in the dark! Not recommended... unless you were constipated then it's highly recommended!

John Curry hadn't changed, his hormones were still percolating in his pants. We all knew what John was like and so did Ken Arey. He approached me and John one evening as we prepared to go out on the town. Ken told John that there was no way he could go out on the town without getting his leg over and made a wager with him. John felt that this was an aspersion upon his good character and took up the challenge. So we departed, with Ken giving me orders to watch him like a hawk. The first bar we went into was John's downfall. We entered the place and sat at the bar ordering our drinks. Before the barman poured them John was attracting a couple of girls looking for 'good time Johnnie'. To be fair, he resisted their charms at first. Then, after about three minutes, he was hooked. He happily went with these two and joined a few more around the corner. I continued to sit at the bar and watched as the drinks he ordered were carefully poured. One, John's, was the real McCoy, while the others were 'cold tea' off the top shelf. We eventually left the bar and I asked John how he was going to explain that to Ken. "Not a problem," he said, "I didn't get a leg over, just got a great hand job!" Next morning Ken Arey came running up to me. "Well?" he asked with some urgency, "Did he?!" I told him he only had a five finger knuckle shuffle. Ken seemed so disappointed; he'd lost his bet on a technicality. "What bar was it?" he asked, hoping to salvage something from his shattered hopes. When I told him the name of the bar Ken perked up then laughed his nuts off. I couldn't really see the joke until Ken told me that the bar concerned was frequented by gays and transvestites No wonder they knew how to pleasure a man, but who was going to tell John?

There was only one purpose to Cliff OP and that was to stand guard in the sentry box, so when we weren't doing that we had to amuse ourselves with other activities like lizard hunting. One of the lads caught a rather large specimen and we thought we'd make a chariot for it. We gathered some scraps of wood, string and a beer can. The plan was to catch more like him and race them, which would keep us happy for hours. First we had to try out our 'test pilot' with his contraption. We placed him on the ground, steadied his chariot and released him. Boy did he shift! He went that fast that none of us could catch him. He went off like a rocket and was never seen again. I don't know how long lizards live for but he probably spent the rest of his life dragging a beer can behind him. I bet that cramped his style in the mating season.

We were on one of our lizard hunts when I espied one of our section giving himself hand relief in the sentry box. I happened to be at the front of the box searching for lizards when I had the idea of popping up in front of the window and pulling a face at the vigilant sentry within. I did pop up and I did pull a face but I never expected to see the sentry mangling his member over a porn magazine! Because his eyes were screwed shut he didn't see me so I bobbed back down again. At this point I should have been discreet about the horrible sight in the sentry box but, instead, I went and told everyone else. Then we all crouched in front of the box and popped up as one. A quick tap on the glass caused the sentry to contort like he was having a heart attack but, amazingly, his grip never diminished and his hand was still going.

The camp shower was a corrugated tin shed and the waste water ran down a pipe to a pit that was covered with a very heavy duckboard. This 'lid' was probably the weight of a battle tank and, therefore, was viewed as an immovable object. For some reason Ben Cartwright, the section arsonist, would pour kerosene down the pipe and ignite it with his ever present lighter. There was no point to this apart from a satisfying 'whoop' sound it made. That was amusing until the day we poured kerosene down it and nobody had a light (Ben was on leave) so I had to run to the kitchen and light a piece of paper. On the third run I managed to keep the paper alight and thrust it at the pipe. Common sense should have told me that fumes had now built up in the pit but common sense had gone on leave that day with Ben. There was the satisfying 'whoop' followed by a nerve shattering 'boom'! The immovable duckboard flew six feet into the air and landed where it wasn't supposed to be. The 'lid' had to be put back in place but my trusted companions had all ran off leaving it to me. With a lot of heaving and a few snapped vertebrae I just about managed it. I heard that Cyprus was supported by three undersea pillars so I was somewhat worried that we'd almost created a second Atlantis.

Being isolated at Cliff OP, we didn't get many visitors but a regular face was that of the local Choggy Wallah. He would often appear on his donkey with his little assistant in tow, always ready to supply us with various commodities. He came in handy when you ran out of cigarettes. He'd jump on his donkey and gallop off to the camp in Kophinou to keep us supplied. One day he decided that we would like a change and came back with Turkish cigarettes, reassuring us that "You like these! They good!" No, they weren't good at all, one drag and it was like inhaling CS gas. It just so happened that we had a tree in the camp, that we labelled 'the hanging tree' because we had a noose dangling from one of its limbs. It was only a little tree but he was only a little Choggy so we decided to hang him. You'll be pleased to hear that we put the noose under his armpits and not around his neck. While he hung helplessly I stole his donkey and did a perimeter patrol of the camp. By the end of it he had sore armpits and I had a sore arse so everything balanced out. The

Choggy also had a slingshot which he was very well practiced with. He would load it with a stone, give it several swings then deliver the missile dead on target. A very impressive feat. One day we had a slight disagreement with him, nothing serious but enough for us to chase him out of camp with a rifle. It wasn't loaded but we threatened to shoot him all the same. But he wasn't easily scared off and he fought back with his slingshot - and that was loaded! The little sod had us taking cover in the rations hut, a corrugated tin shed. The stones flew in like bullets and ricocheted off the walls threatening to maim all of us. In the end he held fire and we all emerged defeated.

Because we didn't have a bar in our little camp we had to make do with having a few cans of beer, normally whilst sitting in Ken Arey's bunk. We were in there one night and he showed us his collection of bugs, all manner of creatures pinned onto the board of a fig.11 target. His latest acquisition was a large May bug that was pinned at the top of the board in pride of place. We sat there drinking and chatting while Ben rolled another cigarette with one hand. Because Ken and Ben were old hands they both had stories to entertain us with. Suddenly the air filled with a droning buzz of a May bug. Nobody was sure how it had got in because the door was firmly shut, then somebody pointed out that the bug, in pride of place on Kens board, had come to life and was in kamikaze mode. We wouldn't have minded a bug but this one had a pin through it and was flying around trying to lance everyone. "We thought it was dead!" we cried to Ken. "So did I!" said Ken as we all vacated the hut. We were lucky really, it could have flown with the board still attached and beat us all to death.

Soon after arriving in Cyprus I had applied for a short secondment to the Medical Centre. While we were at Cliff OP the message came through that I'd been accepted and I would be transferred in the next few days. John Curry decided that we should both go out on the town before my departure so we went into Limassol. But of course, John being John, he had to stop off and have his way with a lady of the night. While he grunted and shunted with his new found friend I sat in the corridor and waited. Whilst waiting I couldn't help but notice the pair of frilly pink knickers on the washing line. "What a souvenir," I mused. After some considerable thought I made my move and snatched the delicate underwear off the line sending a redundant clothes peg whizzing across the floor and under the curtain that separated us. Lucky for me she was too preoccupied to notice. I felt proud to have captured the enemies' colours but, unfortunately, those very same draws would come back and haunt me at the end of the tour. When John finished unstirring his loins we continued piling through the bars. Indeed, we went through so many watering holes that we both ended up with no taxi fare. Even though I was ten sheets to the wind I attempted to draw cartoons of the other drinkers in an effort to make good our finances. Unfortunately they preferred to buy me a drink than give me cash so I ended up totally sloshed and passed out. Nobody could have been more surprised than me the next morning when I woke up in my own bed. How did that possibly happen? The mystery was soon solved when John told me that he had given the taxi driver my watch. Apparently he couldn't bear being parted from his own. I had no chance of getting that back because John couldn't remember what he looked like. But now I was leaving the bosom of B Company and heading for Polemidhia where they would train me to be a brain surgeon...

Chapter 9   Surgical Spirits

February 1973

Polemidhia Camp was home to HQ Company and all of its departments, including the Medical Centre. This is where I met Sergeant Mike Sinden, the medical sergeant. I wasn't sure what he thought of me at the time but he used to grind his teeth every time he walked by. I was also reunited with the MO, Captain Fitzgerald, and L/Cpl Scouse Gidman - the blood sucker. Scouse was RAMC born and bred and he used to disappear at times so he could play rugby. He and I often had shoot-outs with 40 ml syringes at 20 paces, although I thought it was out of order when he rolled up in the early hours of the morning and shot me in my bed. The MO told me to find Scouse one day and I found him in the toilet. "Scouse," I called, "The MO wants you in the office." Scouse gave his response and I hot footed it back to the MO. "He's in the toilet catching fishes Sir," I told him. The MO looked at me gone out but that's what Scouse had said, so I heard. When Scouse did arrive the MO looked at him. "Catching fishes?" he asked. "On the toilet?" Scouse looked at him then looked at me. "Passing faeces you idiot!" he said. Well, it sounded like catching fishes to me.

Most of the routine here was somewhat mundane, dealing with minor ailments and the usual things soldiers go down with to get off parades. But all this brightened up when the Sergeants mess went on a mass diet; obviously someone thought that some of them were getting a little podgy. So it came to pass that I met up with Big Joe K-L again. Because he was someone special to me we used to put the tape measure in the fridge before his arrival. He'd come through the doors and peel off his shirt. Then we'd reach around his ample girth. "Fuck a duck!!" he would cry as we put the tape measure to use. "Have you had that in the fuckin' fridge or fuckin' what!?" Of course we had, but we took a few inches and pounds off in return for our childish prank.

One morning it was my day off so it seemed only right that I should plan my day from the comfort of my pit. My train of thought was interrupted by one of the other orderlies making an entrance. "Quick! Get dressed!" he said, "The MO wants to see you in his office." I quickly threw my uniform on and dashed to the medical centre where I met the MO outside his office. "Russell," he said, "have you ever seen a dead body before?" I confessed that, apart from a poorly looking Bhatta, I hadn't. "Prepare yourself then," he said, "I've got one in the office." Was he winding me up? Were these RAMC scoundrels having a laugh at my expense? I followed Captain Fitzgerald into the office and found it was no joke at all. There, lying very still on a stretcher was the body of a young soldier. His name was Private J.B. Masters and it was 8th February 1973. He had been shot in a shooting accident at one of the locations. On the orders of the MO, myself and another orderly cleaned him up in preparation for the ambulance trip to the Military Hospital in Akrotiri. When we arrived at the hospital the MO took me to one side and told me that I would be in on the autopsy. "I think you'll find it interesting," he said. I'm glad to say that, when the coroner arrived, there wasn't room for me in there. John Masters wasn't the first to become a casualty of a shooting accident and I knew, in my heart, that he certainly wouldn't be the last. I felt it was a sad waste of a young life.

For the rest of us, life went on and someone told me of a bar in Nicosia where the hostess did the most amazing things with key rings. That was Helen's Bar. I was told that she was well endowed in the chest department and could twirl the said key rings on her nipples. Now I'm not one for relying on outrageous rumours so me and a mate went to investigate these claims. Helen was a charming lady in her thirties and sat behind the bar with an air of abandon. Obviously I couldn't just walk in there and say "Hey Helen! Show us your tits!" so we sat down at the bar and had a few brandy sours first. She was a very pleasant woman, chatty and smiling, so after a few drinks I asked her about this party trick of hers. (It never hurt to ask, she could only say no or slap my face off.) As it happened she did neither of those things. Instead she gave a laugh, pulled up her sweater and delved into a drawer for a couple of those key rings. We were both awestruck, hypnotised by the twirling chrome rings that swung on her nipples which were like organ stops. We had a great laugh that night and Helen made a big impression on everyone she met. She was lovely and I certainly will never forget her. Many years later I would meet an old RAF veteran at my local. He knew I'd been to Cyprus and one night, out of the blue, he asked me if I ever went to Helen's Bar. Yes, he'd been there too and he also had fond memories!

Back at the medical centre we continued with the normal routine. One of the orderlies came along and informed me we had a mouse running about in the building so we set about hunting it down. He located it and managed to trap it in a corner with the bristly end of a broom while I ran off and got hold of some ether. That'll slow him up a bit. After a liberal dose of the ether the broom was eased away and Mickey Mouse lay motionless on the tiled floor, out like a light. Sadly we used too much of the knockout stuff and it quickly became apparent that he was the late Mickey Mouse. Dead as a door nail. We were going to operate on it but I don't think that would have achieved much so we put the deceased mouse in a jar. Then we filled it with ether to preserve it. That was a stupid idea - you use formaldehyde to preserve things, not ether! In the end its fur fell out and we had a bald mouse in a jar. I was in the Choggy shop thinking about all of this when I noticed the girl behind the counter, cigarette in her lips and desperately trying to find a light. I suddenly remembered that cool move that Ben Cartwright taught me with a box of matches. I knew that would come in handy! I set the box up in my hand then reached out to the young lady in a suave and seductive manner. Then I flicked the match in a way that couldn't fail to impress her. Well it did fail. As I flicked the match round it continued through its arc until the head of sulphur buried itself into the web between my thumb and index finger. That, I have to say, fucking hurt. I've never tried to repeat that trick again. The girl? She sauntered off with the smell of burnt flesh up her nose and probably gave up smoking. A few weeks earlier we had a casualty come to us with a cut to the head which he accrued in a game of football. I gather he went to head the ball but hit the goalpost instead. It was the MO who put in the sutures because I wasn't qualified to do such things, but I could remove them when the time came and that time was now. I believe his name was Tomlinson, a nice man with a rather quite demeanour. I took him into the treatment room, unwrapped a scalpel and tweezers, and then set about the task. The first one came out of his scalp. "Ouch!" he said rather loudly. Then the second one came out followed by the same reaction. Tut! Tut! I thought what a wimp. By the time I'd finished he was cursing even louder. So what was the problem? Apparently removing stitches from the area of the scalp is a very painful thing. Especially when Russell's on the job! It was about the same time when we received another casualty, a tall and lanky chap called Stretch Turner. He had a bad back and there wasn't much we could do about that except bed him down in the medical centre. Normally that wouldn't be a problem but Stretch was longer than the bed and he had to be laid down flat. After a quick search of the camp we found a plank to slip under his mattress which allowed his feet to overhang the bed. All we had to do now was to wait on him hand and foot and tend to all his needs. Stretch showed his appreciation after his meals by throwing orange peel at us. Not very nice but he was an amusing bloke and kept us happy.

There was more to this medicinal lark than dealing with patients, we also had to keep the place hygienically clean and dispose of any rubbish. (A chance to rid ourselves of Stretch? No, maybe not.) One day we took out the burnable waste and shoved it in the brazier in the yard. Having set light to it we stood watching it. Ben Cartwright would have liked this. Then an undetected aerosol can went 'poof!' and flew out of the fire. "That's interesting," we thought, then imagined what a full aerosol would have done. But why imagine when we had lots of them in the store and time on our hands? So I toddled off and got a full one which we flung into the conflagration. We both took cover and waited for the loud 'poof!' We didn't have to wait long but it wasn't a 'poof' we got. It was a massive bang which threw flaming debris everywhere. Worse than that, the standby platoon was based in the camp and when the bang was heard they were deployed to the town expecting to find a shooting incident! With that, we extinguished the fire and retired to the Choggy shop.

There was another fire one night but nothing to do with us. All the troops were billeted in old wooden huts and our signals platoon was no different. It was their hut that went up in flames for one reason or another so it was all hands to the pump or, in this case, to the fire buckets. Most of the damage should have been contained but every time another bucket went on, the flames grew fiercer. The fire seemed to enjoy having water thrown on it and got more excited with each bucket. Eventually the hut and its contents became a pile of smoking ashes with nothing to salvage. The problem turned out to be the contents of the fire buckets. For years, soldiers had put a film of kerosene on the water within the buckets to keep down the 'mossies' from breeding in there. Although this was done religiously, nobody gave a thought about actually putting water in there. Some changes were quickly made after that night.

My stint with the medical crew was now coming to an end. It had been an interesting time and I enjoyed working with Mike Sinden, Scouse, the MO and the other orderlies but I also missed my mates in 4 platoon, B Company. They had vacated Cliff OP and were now in Airport Camp, Nicosia, which is where we were reunited once more. Airport Camp was a large, sprawling place and was home to all the contingents that made up the UN force. It was in this location where I got my long awaited R and R. This was a few days where we were allowed out in civvies instead of the normal uniform or walking out dress. I didn't actually go anywhere; I just based myself in the camp and would wander out now and again. One night I went over to Nicosia airport, just outside the camp, with Wonky Hibbert. We both sat at the bar knocking back ouzos until our eyesight dimmed and then we crawled back to camp on our elbows. When I got back to the room I met Andy Hawker who was looking dreadful. It may have been the ouzo or he may well have looked dreadful. "I'm not well John," he said. He didn't look good so I told him to go sick in the morning. "But I'm on guard duty in 10 minutes," he replied. Then he asked me if I would do his guard duty for him. "Don't talk wet," I told him, "I've been out with Wonky! I'm pissed as a fart!" Andy squinted at me and offered me 200 cigarettes, a common currency in these parts. As if I could be so easily bought. 10 minutes later I was in Andy's uniform and standing on stag at the gates. This probably wasn't the best idea I've ever had but when you've got ouzo coursing through your brain, anything seems like a good idea. Because it was cold in the early hours we wore parkas so I was able to disguise myself with the hood. The bloke on duty waffled away to his heart's content, Andy this and Andy that. Blah, blah blah. Luckily the hood muffled most of the drivel although sewing the hood closed was a good option. Relief came when the Land Rover arrived and I went mobile which meant I could sit in warm comfort and be driven around the camp. This was quite nice really until the radio came to life. We were told that some poor squaddie had got a bed job and we were to rush to the scene. (A bed job was when you got beaten up in your bed.) We arrived at the location and the driver decided he would attend while I manned the radio. Fine by me, it saved me staggering around the place. After a few minutes I happened to notice a window open in the cookhouse so I wandered across to take a peek, bearing in mind that the perpetrator of the bed job was still at large. The window was barred but, if I was really careful, I could just squeeze my head through. I knew I shouldn't have been there and I was half pissed but sometimes you have to do the right thing. I just about managed to get my head through and peered around in the darkness of the kitchen. That's when I saw him! About 7 feet tall with a cleaver in his hand! I very nearly ripped my ears off when I pulled my head out of the bars and ran to the radio. With official radio procedure thrown out of the window I called for assistance and the rest of the guard were there in minutes. With keys rattling they opened up the cookhouse and we all entered with torches flashing all over the place. Suddenly one of the guard called from the kitchen. "Quick! Over here!" he shouted, "Give me a hand with this brute!" We all ran towards the voice and found the sentry shining his torch onto a set of cooks whites and a row of utensils hanging up alongside. Lucky for me everyone was too busy taking the piss to notice that I should never have been there.

It was in Airport Camp that I got a touch of toothache. The dentist at Bassingbourn had filled it but he did say that it may have to come out one day. Well it was giving me grief so I guess that day had arrived. I got driven to the UN dental centre and met the dentist, a very stern looking Austrian officer. "In der seat!" he commanded. I obeyed promptly. "Open der mouth!" he said. Again I complied. I felt that if I didn't play along it would the firing squad. He climbed into my mouth and poked roughly about. After some deliberation he decided "It vill have to kom out!" I rather expected that, I just didn't expect to be treated by Joseph Mengele. He unrolled his wallet of instruments and I swear I saw a swastika enamelled on each of the handles. He pulled out a tool that looked like a bradawl and set about attacking the tooth. As I admired his duelling scar he did his best to break the tooth up, and because it was in my top set he was almost lifting me out of the seat. Then he went in with a pair of pliers and emerged with a big tooth. Shit, they don't look that big when they're in your gums. At least it's over I thought. "Und now for der little pieces!" he said and climbed back in. I eventually escaped although I was minus one tooth and had a longer neck. The dentist just rolled up his tools and was probably reminiscing about the day that Adolf Hitler had presented them to him at the Wolf's Lair.

"Mein Gott! Is der big bugger!"

As soon as the horse tranquilliser had worn off and I got some sort of feeling back in my face I went out on the town with my old mate John Curry. He was eager for a drink or ten and his loins were restless again. Bill Kempton and a few others came along and we piled into the first bar with the intention of drinking it dry. After necking a few brandy sours a young girl came our way and seemed strangely attracted to me. Was she pissed too? I had a few more Keo brandies and I found myself strangely drawn to her. Bill decided it was time to move onto the next bar but I disagreed, I could be onto a winner here. Although I was pissed I vaguely remember that she led me by the hand up a spiral stair case and, with a prompt from her, I gave her some money for a bottle of 'something special'. While she was on this errand I fished out a condom from my pocket and peeled it out of its wrapper. See, even though I was sloshed, I still remembered the MOs wise words. As I fumbled about trying to get this bloody thing on my uncooperative member, Bill came up the stairs. "C'mon!" he said, "We're going now!" I protested strongly saying that the young lady hadn't come back with that bottle of 'something special' yet. Bill dragged me to my feet, wherever they were.

"Don't you know when you've been conned?" he said with no compassion whatsoever. Apparently not. The night wore on and I became worn out. We all managed to get separated and I ended up with John Curry. Whereas I was ready to go back to camp, John's hormones were just waking up and he had an uprising in his pants. Needless to say he found a 'companion' and I was left in the hallway again. But at least I had company this time, an old Mama, all wrinkled and about 200 years old. She sat there knitting, probably knitting a new skin, and watched me through slit-like eyes. Maybe she'd heard about my shenanigans with knickers on clothes lines. After about 15 minutes of me and the turtle staring each other out, a voice emanated from the room. "Enough Johnnie! You finish now! You too long time!!" Obviously John wanted his money's worth. But the salamander sitting opposite me decided he'd had enough. She plonked her knitting down and went into the room, dragging her skin behind. She emerged with John's clothes and threw them in the street. I sat there bemused by this turn of events when John appeared in his shirt and socks. "Get me clothes!" he pleaded. I refused, because to see John going out into the street half naked would be something to write home about. This I had to see. Unfortunately so did the passing Army patrol. Luckily they were Australians, and so, after a lot of taking the piss, they gave us a lift back to camp. And I got to keep my new watch.

Cyprus was a great experience. Over the last 6 months, lots had happened and the caricatures that I drew should have got me shot at dawn. Major Crumley, the OC, would never had seen his but it appeared in the Queen's Journal. It didn't help that he became my target at the Christmas show! 'Lamb-chop' Russell - no relation - got steaming drunk one night and ended up naked in the perimeter fence of the camp where he 'found' religion. A funny place to find it but there's all sorts in those fences. But the tour was now at an end and we were all lined up on the runway, the whole Battalion, waiting for the ground staff to check our luggage to ensure there were no aerosols or other dangerous items in there. When it came to me, the RAF NCO bravely plunged his hand into my laundry bag then pulled out a pair of pink frilly knickers, those same ones I liberated months before. If that wasn't bad enough he waved them over his head so everyone could see. "They're battle honours!" I protested.

Chapter 10 Rocking

May 1973

We got back to Tidworth then took a few weeks leave where I did the usual thing, having a few beers with family and friends, but this time I had a healthy tan. Then I caught the coach at the fire station and made the journey back to Lucknow Barracks. When I arrived there I had to chuckle, the lads had been busy and placed someone's complete bed space on the balcony. The bed was there, locker, bedside table and even the mat. What a laugh. I walked into the barrack room and found my bed space totally empty. I stood on the balcony, got undressed, put my stuff in my locker and crawled into my bed. And that's where I stayed until reveille. I'd seen worse, someone once came back off the piss and went to bed. They lifted his bed, with him in it, and moved it onto the parade square complete with his locker and bed side mat. He looked stunned when the regimental police woke him up in the morning! Our stay in Tidworth would be a short one because we had another posting which would send us abroad: Gibraltar. A lump of rock on the tail end of Spain. In the meantime we still had physical training because we were soldiers. Someone had the great idea of going for a run up Sudbury Hill, a silly idea that just knackered us all. (We called it 'Sodbury' Hill and soldiers still do apparently!) Then someone else had a better idea: run to the YMCA, have a coffee and a cheese roll, and then run back to camp. Much more civilised. Steve Terry was still with our platoon and he and his wife invited me out to their place for dinner and a few beers. Because the Battalion had a large married group there weren't enough quarters to go around so Steve and his wife were living in a mobile home the other side of Stonehenge. It was only a bus ride away so it wasn't a problem getting there. We had dinner and a couple of beers and it turned out to be a very pleasant visit. Then I had to say goodbye and catch the last bus home. It was only a twenty minute journey and I shared the bus with four soldiers from another unit who were armed with jugs of scrumpy. At first they were drinking it themselves then they offered the bus driver some. (I'm glad to say that he declined!) Then they spotted me at the back of the bus. "You'll have some won't you mate!" they called. Well why not, I'd only had two cans and I didn't want to refuse their hospitality and upset them, so I joined them. Surely it couldn't do any harm over a twenty minute journey? The bus arrived at Lucknow and I fell out of the door. I must have looked a right sight trying to get to my barrack room...

It was here that one of the lads, Bob Tufnell, decided he was getting married so it was only right to give him a send-off on the morning of his wedding. Most of it was shaking hands and back slapping but someone decided to give him a hug followed by a love bite on his neck. Explain that on your wedding night! I think, if I ever got married, I'd keep it quiet.

September 1973

The RAF kindly transported us once again to a warmer climate: Gibraltar. Because it was the RAF we weren't allowed through Spanish air space so it took a little longer than a normal civvy flight. A small price to pay for going abroad again. Landing in Gib was a cross fingered affair because it was a slip of a runway that poked out into the sea. To be fair there wasn't anywhere else you could really put an air strip because the rest of the rock was pretty much full. Home for B Company was South Barracks, an old colonial building that smelled of pirates. Further up the hill was Lathbury Barracks, somewhat more modern and comfortable and home to HQ Company. Perhaps I was due a transfer? For B Company it was to be constant square bashing in readiness for ceremonial duties which meant being issued with white tunics and blues trousers. I never got to wear mine. They had decided that only smart soldiers would be considered for these special duties so me and other 'not so smart' soldiers were relegated to camp guard and border guard duties. On the plus side I wasn't required to march up and down with a shiny bayonet and twat hat, which meant that I could concentrate on other things, like the pubs. And what an abundance of pubs, every other building seemed to be a watering hole and, with the variety of opening hours, you could drink all through the weekend if you wanted to! I thought I'd died and gone to heaven.

There was a bar in one of the many side streets and it had a real live parrot in the open window. Being attracted to this exotic bird, John Curry and I went in. John was really missing the delights of Cyprus so this exotic bird would have to do. We got a beer each and sat by this bird, admiring its colourful plumage, when two girls walked in. The parrot gave such an ear-piercing wolf whistle that our ear drums almost burst. Then the two girls looked in our direction where the whistle came from. If looks could kill they would have blown us out of our boots. We were told of another pub where, it was rumoured, the barmaid wore a short skirt and no draws. As I've said before I never take rumours at face value so John and I paid a visit there. We arrived at the bar and promptly ordered drinks off the bottom shelf. Because it was a short skirt we ordered off the top shelf too. We both ended up out of our skulls but it was true, the poor girl couldn't afford underwear.

Jack Sear and Charlie Williamson were still with us and they were fun to go out drinking with. They were like me, go out, have a laugh and go home. We didn't want to fight with anyone, life is too short for that game. We came back off the beer in the early hours of one morning and we were well and truly 'merry'. So merry that Jack and Charlie thought it would be a good idea to throw me off the first floor balcony where our barrack room was. Unfortunately, a few doors away, it was the room of Corporal Alan Thubron and he wasn't too pleased about be woken up by drunks. Mainly because he was the duty cook in the morning which meant an early enough start as it was. He was clearly upset about having his sleep disturbed and put the three of us on a charge. Next morning Jack, Charlie, me, Corporal Thubron and the Provost Sergeant stood outside the OCs office. Alan Thubron was there because he was levelling the charge against us and the Provost Sergeant was there in case the three defendants turned nasty I suppose. We were swiftly marched in at the double and halted in front of Major Gordon Crumley's desk. The old Major looked up and cast his eye over the three shame faced soldiers in front of him. He read out our names, ranks, and numbers (just to make sure he had the right ones) then read out the charge. "How do you plead Russell?" he asked. "Guilty Sir!" I replied in a soldier-like fashion. "Williamson?" "Guilty Sir!" replied Charlie. "How about you Sear?" he said turning his gaze to Jack. "Guilty Sir!" came the standard reply. There was no point in denying it, we were all there and we knew we had been naughty. The Major pored over the paperwork before him and deliberated over the punishment. "Now I know you boys," he said at length, "and I know you are not the drinking sort." I could hear Jack stifling a laugh. "So knowing you like I do," the Major said, "case dismissed." We were all ordered to about turn and marched out at the double, disbelief on our faces. But that was nothing compared to the look on Corporal Thubron's face. But that wasn't the end of it. A few nights later the three of us came back from the town, after a bellyful of beer, and we were as quiet as church mice. More or less. At least quiet enough to sneak up to Corporal Thubron's door where we decided to give him his early morning call - three hours early. I crept up to his bedside and give him a nudge. "Corporal Thubron," I said, in a disguised whisper, "Your early morning call." He shuffled under his sheets, mumbled then asked for the book to sign. Oh shit, I'd forgotten about the book! With the plan unravelling fast I rapidly beat a retreat from his room. "Hang on!" I heard him shout. "I'm not the duty cook today!" (In 2015 I attended a reunion and met Alan dressed in his Chelsea Pensioners red coat. I had a great chat with him and confessed my sins. We were still talking about it over breakfast the next morning!)

At some point Sergeant Major Alan Prince left us for D Company and was replaced by Sergeant Major Patterson. He was a big man but seemed a reasonable sort, until the day he returned to his office and found Snowball sitting in his chair with his feet on his desk. "Snowball!" he bellowed, "Get your boots off my desk and your arse out of my chair!!" "Mr Snowball to you," he replied. There was a scuffle and the CSM threw Snowball out onto the veranda. Words were exchanged and Snowball stormed off to his room, only to appear with a pile of his kit and proceeded to set fire to it. Needless to say Snowball was arrested and carted away, never to be seen again. We think he'd had enough of the Army and worked his ticket. It happens occasionally.

In those days long gone we were still using pay books. Every Friday the paymaster would come down to South Barracks with his escort and set himself up in a room, cash meticulously laid out on the desk and then he would call each of us in, in alphabetical order of course. We would march in, stamp our feet to attention and present our pay books. He would then sign your book and present you with your wage. This system worked well, week after week, without a hitch. But we still had the soldiers who were practising their drill for the ceremonial duties and we had one turn up at pay parade with his shiny ammo boots. Very commendable, but not the best footwear when you march onto the polished wooden floor of the paymasters temporary office. The soldier briskly marched in and came to a halt, or he would have done if not for his studded boots. He slid ungracefully into the desk and the cash flew in all directions! Panic ensued with the paymaster and his escort herding everyone out so they could gather the notes and loose change together. It was some time before anyone else got paid. The sliding soldier? Well he was put to the back of the queue.

South Barracks pay parade ... with ammo boots!

December 1973

Christmas Day came and, although not as hot as Cyprus, was fairly warm and I found myself on guard duty at South Barracks. No 'gunfire' for me then. It was a relaxed guard and the guard commander was pretty easy going this day. He decided it wouldn't hurt that evening if a few of us popped over to The George Elliot pub across the road. So we pulled straws and it turned out that I would look after the guard room while the rest of them went for a pint. Someone was supposed to come back and let me loose but, strangely, that never happened. So I sat there, at the desk, with a bottle of beer under the counter. Probably the only 'almost' alert sentry in the world. Just as I was getting used to my solitude the duty officer hovered into view. Oh shit! "Is the guard commander around?" he asked. I felt like saying 'I'm afraid not Sir, he's over the pub getting rat arsed but if you pop over there I'm sure he'll buy you a pint because the twat didn't buy me one!' But I resisted because I didn't want to be labelled a low life for the rest of my career. "He's just got his head down Sir." I lied, indicating the empty beds in the back room. "Could you give him a nudge please?" he asked. I'd look stupid marching over to the pub to deliver the nudge so, instead, I went into the empty room and pretended to nudge the sleeping Corporal. "I'm afraid he's flat out Sir, he's been on the go all day." The duty officer looked disappointed. "That's a pity," he said, "Could you give him this when he awakens?" He then placed a bottle of whisky on the counter. "My pleasure Sir." I said taking the bottle. Well, some of it would be my pleasure. The remainder of the guard returned in the early hours pissed as farts and went to bed. Meanwhile my cartoons were about to open new doors for me...

I was told that the Battalion signwriter was coming to the end of his service and a replacement was required so someone suggested that I should apply because of my artistic talents. So I did and within days I was relocated in Lathbury Barracks to the Quartermasters department. Now I didn't have to worry about my white tunic anymore because I could wear the coveted brown dust coat that singled you out as a member of the QMs. I may have looked an 'orrible sight but I was the battalion signwriter! The battalion only had one CO, one RSM and it had one signwriter. What a delightful position to be in. Moving to Lathbury Barracks did have its drawbacks, up until now I was only under the watchful eye of B Company but now I was under the constant glare of anybody and everybody in the upper echelons of HQ Company. There were Senior NCOs, Sergeant Majors and Officers all over the place and they all seemed to watch your every move. At least that's how I felt. But I made new friends here in the Pioneer department. Corporal Bill Dixon, Barry Hemsley, Zip Nolan, Dave Gray and Eric Dennis were the craftsmen I worked with. Bill Dixon was in charge of us and he was an excellent carpenter. Barry was another chippie while Dave was the plumber and Eric a painter. I can't remember what Zip did apart from drink a lot. At the head of this little band was Sergeant Major Mick Aylward. Bill came into my little cubby hole of a workshop one day and told me that the Sergeant Major would 'love a cup of tea'. I took that as Bill ordering me to make a cup of tea for him. This would be an easy task if I had tea bags, but all we had was loose tea. If my mum was there she would have produced a tea strainer out of thin air but she wasn't there and there was no strainer. Not to be foiled by this minor detail I set about making a tea bag. Using improvisation I took an old pair of long johns out of the rag box and cut a square out of them. I poured a suitable amount of tea leaves on this patch and tied it up with string. Voilà! One tea bag manufactured out of next to nothing. The tea was made and I proudly presented it to the Sergeant Major. I cracked on with my signwriting and within two minutes Bill came crashing through the door. "Good God man!" he shrieked, "Are you trying to poison the Sergeant Major or what!?" I looked at Bill then I looked at what appeared to be a thirst quenching cuppa that he was gripping. I couldn't see a problem but it was clear that Bill and the Sergeant Major didn't share my view. "Taste it!!" Bill yelled. I told Bill that I'd rather not, I'm a coffee drinker. I'm glad to say that the Sergeant Major survived the toxic tea bag incident and a court martial never looks good on your Army record.

That box of rags proved very useful where my imagination was concerned. The odd bits of material were obtained from the clothing stores; things like shirts and long johns which were past their best and handed in for exchange. The staff there worried that we would take these then try and exchange them again for new gear so they would slash the old clothing to stop us doing that. That's fine, to me a slashed shirt was a gift. With some cardboard, a splodge of maroon paint and some plastic wood I found I could conjure up a very impressive exit wound in the back of one of those shirts. It looked suitably gruesome when you wore it. At the time of doing that, the QM tasked us to make a guy for the local school bonfire which happened to coincide with an internal security exercise on the camp. So we got an old set of coveralls and stuffed it with paper and other combustible material. One of the lads thought it would be funny if we stuck my 'exit wound shirt' on it while someone else thought it was even funnier to display the finished thing and drape it over the 'Internal Exercise in progress' sign that stood outside the workshop. It did look the part if I say so myself. But these exercises are run by a group of officers known collectively as exercise control and it's they who decide what direction the exercise takes, not the signwriter. They were very surprised to hear of a 'fatality' over the air waves when a passing patrol spotted our guy. I was called to the QMs office and he pointed out the error of my ways.

The Quarter Master was Captain P.A. Newman, an eccentric kind of officer who had risen through the ranks and this would be the first of many visits to his office. Barry Hemsley was summoned to the QMs house one day; the wardrobe needed a new rail. But not any old rail, this was about fifteen feet long and was needed to accommodate the Captain's many uniforms that he had accumulated during his service. So Barry obliged and fitted the new rail then had the job of putting all this clobber onto coat hangers and hanging them in place. He was only a few uniforms away from finishing when the whole lot collapsed under the weight and landed in a very un-regimental heap on the wardrobe floor. Barry was quick to remedy the situation and the Captain never got to hear about the lapse.

Captain Newman was a stickler for regimental traditions and history, so when two old naval cannons were dredged up off the sea bed in the docks he claimed them for Queen and country. The governor of Gibraltar would have liked them but the Captain would have none of that - they were British! Bill and Barry spent hours working on two wooden carriages to support these relics and both were installed either side of the parade square. But the QM wasn't satisfied with that, he wanted them to fire blue and orange smoke across the square (blue and orange were the battalion colours). This dubious task was left to Bill and me. We decided that a thunderflash would sort the bang side of things out although the blue and orange smoke was another matter. We agreed that two tins of watercolour powder would produce the colours but, we both agreed, it wouldn't amount to anything more than a cloud the colour of, well, shit really. But we gave it a whirl anyway even it was just to prove a point. We commenced this operation under the baleful eye of Captain Newman and his entourage. We struck the thunderflash and threw it down the barrel followed immediately by the two bags of powder paint. There was a loud bang and a cloud of shit coloured smoke hung in the air, just as we predicted. The Captain wandered back to his office and we wandered off back to the drawing board. We both came up with plan B - coloured toilet rolls! With any luck they would both go like streamers across the parade square. Bill and I stood either side of the old cannon and watched Captain Newman and his followers approach. There was also a Company Sergeant Major taking his men through a slow march routine on the square but we took little notice of that. Bill explained to the QM what we were about to do and what we hoped to achieve and the approval was given. The thunderflash, having been struck, was thrust down the barrel. Two coloured toilet rolls were put in and tamped down with a modified broom handle. Within seconds the cannon shuddered with the explosion and rolls flew out with considerable velocity. None of us could have imagined the range of a smouldering toilet roll but it did cause the marching company to break into a very quick march to avoid the missiles. Because he was Captain Newman nobody complained, they all knew what he was like. After that the plan was shelved until someone could come up with a better idea. They never did.

"Make a note Russell, loo roll - 250 metres"

Our painter, Eric Dennis, would rather go fishing than drinking so I thought it would make a change for me when he invited me to tag along. We had his mate Clive with us and decided to paddle a rubber dinghy out to the detached mole, but this required three trips. Eric would paddle out there first with me and some of the fishing gear, then I would paddle back. Then Clive would get in and paddle to the mole with me and the rest of the gear. That was a good plan, so good it nearly worked. It all seemed to fall apart when Clive started the last leg of the trip. Initially he started OK but then a huge passenger liner decided to make its move too. The loud hooter sounded and I looked over Clive's shoulder to see the huge ship pulling away from its berth, its propellers angrily churning up the water. Didn't the ship's captain have wing mirrors or a crow's nest? Clive looked behind and his eyes very nearly popped from their sockets, neither of us had seen a ship this close before! It looked like a huge steel skyscraper moving through the water. Clive put more effort into his paddling, which would have been a good thing but he only had one paddle in the water and we went in a tight circle. As the ship came closer our circle became smaller. I felt I would rather die drunk on dry land than sober at sea! Soon the big ship pulled away, Clive got both paddles in the water and we made it to the detached mole leaving us both alive to tell the tale.

Gibraltar was populated by all sorts of people including Moroccans and I met one while waiting in a bar for a friend of mine. I ordered a pint and watched this bloke with his beer and a plate of snails. He'd have a sip of his beer then pick up a snail on a cocktail stick which he happily consumed. He saw me looking, then offered me one. "No thanks," I told him, "not my thing really." I continued waiting for my mate, who was obviously delayed, and ordered another pint, then another one. At this stage my new Moroccan companion got himself another plate of gastropods. After several of these slimy things slid down his throat he turned to me again offering a snail on a stick. "Go on," he urged, "Try one, you like!" I looked at him and thought 'ah, why not?' "You no chew, just swallow," he told me. I took his advice, and the snail, and swallowed it. There was no taste and no sensation. So there was no point really, except that I could say I ate a snail. Why I would want to say that, I've no idea...

As I said earlier I was now under the hard gaze of all at HQ Company so I suppose it was inevitable that I would find myself in trouble one day, they had eyes like shit house spiders. I can't remember what the first charge was. It was probably something that would be viewed as minor in Civvy Street but in the Army any misdemeanour was seen as a heinous offence. Whatever it was I found myself outside the OCs office with Sergeant Major Riddlestone-Holmes escorting me. The OC of HQ

Company was Major Dicky Waite, another officer that came up through the ranks. I was marched in at double time and halted at his desk. "Are you 24281225 Pte Russell?" he asked. He knew I was because I'd drawn a cartoon of him in Cyprus and it was framed on his wall in my line of sight. "Yes Sir!" I replied. He read out the charge, gave me 7 days RPs and the Sergeant Major double marched me out of the office. RPs are 'restriction of privileges' which means attending the guard room after the evening meal and given menial tasks to do while your mates are on the town. Then, at 22:00 hrs you parade at the guard room in your No2s for inspection. And there was no drinking! That was probably a good thing. 7 days of RPs seemed to be the norm, there was no sliding scale. Every time I went in front of Major Waite I came out with seven. I ended up with so many I became known as the RP king, well-deserved if I say so myself.

I was on one run of RPs alongside Barry Hemsley, he must have been a naughty soldier too, and one night they ordered us to strip the paint off the main staircase in the HQ block and repaint them. Scraping these stone steps seemed a lot like hard work (which it was meant to be) so I had the idea of slipping over to the workshops and picking up some paint stripper. That would certainly speed the process up. But the Army was always busy and so were these stairs, officers and SNCOs up and down them all evening. Undeterred, we got on with the job and slopped paint stripper liberally over the steps. Occasionally we had to warn people using the stairs but, being senior, they mostly ignored us. So we gave up telling them in the end. Sergeant Major Perryman was a likeable bloke, he was known as 'ten-to-two feet' due to his stance. Sadly he was the next one to approach the stairs and received no warning from us. The first couple of steps he managed without incident but then he lost it, his legs developed a life of their own and went all akimbo. His pace stick went in one direction and his clip board in the other, such style and grace we'd never seen before. "What the fuck is this!?" he said after landing on his rear end. "That's paint stripper Sir," we told him. He stood up and shot off, like a toilet roll fired out of a cannon, and ran to the men's room. I had horrible visions of the Sergeant Major sitting in the sink with his legs dangling over the side and taps gushing. As far as I know there were no long term effects but Barry had recurring nightmares for weeks. Corporal Bill Dixon was deservedly promoted to Sergeant and called us all into the office to announce his good fortune. "From now on," he said "It's not Bill, it's not Sarge, its Sergeant. Got it?" "Right you are Bill," we all chorused. "As long as you all know," he said and sent us back to work. The truth is that later on in life it would prove useful having Bill in the Sergeants Mess.

Once again I stood outside the OCs office with Sergeant Major Riddlestone-Holmes on yet another 'minor' offence. He double marched me in and halted me at the COs desk where I caught it with my knee. Major Waite straightened out his pens, put his ink pots in order and then started the proceedings. "Are you 24281225 Pte Russell?" he asked. I'm pretty sure he had a good idea it was me, we'd met here before. "Yes Sir!" I replied, looking at that familiar cartoon of him on the wall. "Look me in the eye!" he commanded. Well, that was easier said than done because I was told he had a glass eye, so I stood there looking from one eye to the other, wondering which one was the glass eye. He read out the charge, something about not handing in my weapon ancillaries, considered me guilty and awarded me seven days RPs. The Sergeant Major ordered me to about turn and marched me out. "Fackin' idiot!" he yelled, "If you didn't kick his desk you would have got off with that one!" I didn't believe that for a minute, if I took him a cup of tea I'd march out with RPs. He saved them up for me.

Sergeant Major 'Noddy' Riddlestone-Holmes was a wonderful bloke, short in stature but large in life. It was he who took us HQ newbies onto the square and taught us to drill with the SMG. Having shown us the basics, he stood us at ease which involved having the weapon at an angle across your chest. He marched up and down, explaining the next move, when he noticed that my weapon had sagged somewhat. Without a pause he went past me and swung his pace stick which caught me on the knuckles. "Ouch! Bastard!" I squealed. More out of shock rather than insulting the Sergeant Major. "You don't call me a bastard," he said calmly, "you only think it Russell." Then he continued on with the lesson. The reason for this drill practice was the forthcoming parade where the whole Battalion would be on the square with the Regimental band and Drums. It wouldn't do to have the likes of Russell letting the side down. When the day of the parade came we were all formed up and marched onto the square. There was a long drawn out inspection followed by a pleasant march around the square, accompanied by the stirring music of the band. When they went into the Regimental March (Sussex by the Sea) the Sergeant Major puffed out his chest. "Sing my boys!" he shouted over the music, "Sing at the top of your lungs!" So we did. Then he reached through the ranks and hit me on the head with his pace stick. "Not you Russell," he said. It might have been because I didn't have a singing voice but it was most likely because I only knew the naughty words.

Eric and I spent another night on the detached mole, minus Clive. He didn't come because he had gone off the sea for some reason. There was an abundance of Conga eels in these waters and the keen anglers amongst us made it their goal to land the biggest one they could. Eric was no different and this night he struck lucky. Having spent hours dangling his hook in the sea, the line suddenly went taut and his rod bent violently, then after some hard work on his part we saw the Conga eel break the surface. It looked like a rather large specimen. "Get ready to grab it!" called Eric as he struggled to bring it level with us. Then he swung it in. "Grab it!" he shouted. I have to say that the eel looked big when I was looking down on it and now it was coming in my direction it looked even bigger. It was bigger than me! As the squirming monster lashed about on the line I took evasive action and ducked. The slimy thing passed me by and slapped Eric in the spine. Eric wasn't too pleased with me but I thought it was hilarious and laughed my tits off.

Sometime after that I was in Lathbury Barracks serving another seven days of RPs when Noddy Riddlestone-Holmes approached me in the workshop. He took me to one side and told me that the Sergeants Mess were having a Horror Night the following Friday and he wanted me to do his makeup. Strangely enough Noddy, who was a short bloke, planned on going as Frankenstein's monster. (He had already roped Barry Hemsley in to make him a pair of boots built out of coffee tables!) I told him I would have done but I would still be on RPs that night. "I'll sort that out," he said, "and I'll get you a few beers in!" Well there was something to look forward to. The day before the Horror Night shenanigans Bill came up to me, they had put hessian up all round the walls and needed me to spray paint ghosts and ghoulies up there. I told him the same that I had told Noddy, explaining I was still on RPs. "Leave that to me," he said. So that night I stood outside the guardroom at 18:00 hrs and waited to be detailed off to a job. The Regimental Policeman stood in front of me and eyed me up and down. "You're to report to the Sergeants Mess," he told me and sent me up the road. When I arrived at the Mess I was given cans of luminous spray paint and told what to do. While I beavered away with my graffiti the Mess waiter would bring the occasional beer. "Courtesy of Sergeant Dixon," he would say and saunter off. Luckily the work took me past the 22:00 hrs show parade so it didn't matter that I smelled of beer. The following night I reported to the gatehouse at 18:00 hrs where the Regimental Policeman detailed me off to the Sergeants Mess once more. "Report to Sergeant Major Riddlestone-Holmes," he growled. The Mess waiter showed me to the Sergeant Major's room and when I went in I couldn't help but notice the numerous cartoons of mine on his wall. I then began to apply his makeup and, as I did, I mentioned the works of art that adorned his walls. "I wonder who pinched them," I said. An eye peered out of the makeup. "Rank has its privileges!" he told me. Then, with his makeup done, he hobbled off to the bar wearing his size 20 coffee tables. Oh yes, a few beers were had too.

So the Sergeants Mess had their Horror Night and I just had my RPs to get on with. Or did I? Bill came up to me one morning in the workshop. "Do you know, John," he said, "I nearly gave up drinking last night." I never thought I would hear a statement like that from Bill but then he explained that he was the last one in the bar the previous night when the Mess waiter turned the main lights out. "All I could see was ghosts and ghoulies coming out of the walls!" Apparently my handy work with the spray paint went through the hessian. Nobody noticed in the daylight but the luminous paint came to life in the dark. Then he told me I would have to repaint the walls. I said that painting his walls would be a bit awkward at the moment because of those wretched RPs. "I'll sort that out," he said. That night, outside the guardroom, the Regimental Policeman came along and, reluctantly, detailed me off to the Sergeants Mess. He was beginning to wonder if I was actually on RPs at all. He also got one of the other naughty soldiers to assist me. As we walked up the hill, the lad told me he was a little worried about this. "Do you drink beer?" I asked him. "Yeah," he said, looking a little puzzled. "Then trust me," I said, "you'll like this." The pair of us took the rollers and paint and began our task, with beers coming along freely. By the time the bar was closing we had finished. Bill and Noddy came in to inspect our work. They liked it very much but 'don't the other room look tatty now'. The following night, me and my little helper were painting again and the beer was plentiful.

The next morning would be my last on RPs, they had finally come to an end. Unfortunately I was a tad late getting to the guardroom. I knew that because the Regimental Policeman, Corporal Martin Mills, was marching the prisoners back from breakfast. I went into the guardroom and reported to the guard commander who ticked me off his list. Then just as I was about to walk out Martin Mills came in with his prisoners. "Russell!" he yelled, "Get up those stairs and pick yourself a cell!!" I knew Corporal Mills and thought he was having a laugh, so I asked him if I could have one with a bay window overlooking the Mediterranean. "Get up those fackin' stairs NOW!" he ordered. So he wasn't having a laugh then. Within the hour Sergeant Major Riddlestone-Holmes was double marching me into the COs office once again. I emerged with another cluster of RPs, seven of course. I hadn't even finished the ones I was doing! Worse than that, there were no perks during this lot so I just had to get on with them. But I did see something on the Company notice board, they were looking for ushers. Apparently The Barron Knights were appearing in the town and the Battalion required bodies to usher the squaddies in. I reported to Sergeant Major Noddy and volunteered. He thought that it was very commendable of me, then realised I was still on RPs. "Fack orf!" he said. So, no sorting it out then? That was a shame, I liked The Barron Knights.

The last day of those RPs came and I made a special effort on my turnout for the 22:00 hrs parade. My No2s were pressed, my boots were super shiny and I even polished the brass backing plates on my collar dogs. I wouldn't normally go that mad because, with RPs, I would have been on again the following night anyway. But this was my last night and tomorrow night I'd be out on the lash with my mates. Off I went to the guardroom and joined the line-up. The duty Officer and Battalion Orderly Sergeant arrived, the bugler sounded the last post and the inspection came. The duty officer moved along the line of men, a little bit of adjustment here, some words of encouragement there. Then he came to me. "You look like a bag of shit tied in the middle!" he said, "Battalion Orderly Sergeant!" "Yes Sir!" "Show parade for this man tomorrow night!" "Yes Sir!" Boy was I pissed off. But that, I'm told, is the way the cookie crumbles...

That run of RPs came to an end and, it just so happened John Curry joined me in HQ Company as a cook (or 'Chef' as he liked us to refer to him). So we both went out on the town where we met a lovely lady serving behind one of the bars. She was married to one of the Royal Engineers and always cheered us up, especially when she produced a Jews Harp from behind the bar. She played it and we were suitably impressed. John, not one to miss an opportunity to improve his social standing, decided to have a go at this small instrument. He sat on his bar stool, placed the instrument to his lips and gave it a twang. Actually it was less of a twang and more of a 'thung' on account that he caught his tongue in it. A short squeal was followed by some unintelligible words and, after some guffawing from me and the engineer's wife, we released him from the instrument's grip. We thought it was hilarious but John disagreed, although it was difficult to establish that because we couldn't understand a word he said for the next half hour.

The Key and Anchor was another bar that I used to frequent and the man who ran it was also called John, a very good-humoured man who loved my cartoons (even though they were only drawn on beermats!) At one stage my artistic beermats covered the wall behind the bar. It was like the Tate art gallery of Gibraltar. I sat at the bar one day and he showed me a photograph of a voluptuous woman and I asked him "Is that the wife?" He laughed his head off. "No!" he said, "It's him at the end of the bar!" I looked down the bar and there was this bloke, pint in one hand and holding onto the leash of an Alsatian, looking very... glam I suppose. "You're kidding me!" I said. But no, he wasn't. Welcome to the world of gays and transvestites in Gib. They were a small and exclusive group that usually used a bar called The Hole in the Wall. Naturally! John Curry and I were in the Key and Anchor one night and got to know these people and they were very entertaining. I quickly pointed out to them that I was absolutely straight as an arrow. "Nobody's perfect," one of them replied. But they were great company to drink with. One of them ran the Oliver Twist bar - although we cruelly called it the Twisted Oliver - and he always seemed happy and carefree. We were in the Oliver Twist one night and a Navy ship was in port, sailors were everywhere. I would have thought that Oliver would be over the moon with all of these matelots about but he appeared depressed and deeply unhappy. It didn't help when three sailors came in and took the piss out of him. They grabbed their beers and sat by the open window that looked into the street while the simmering Oliver stormed out to the back. The sailors continued with their banter and didn't seem to notice Oliver appear in the window behind them. He reached in, hauled one of them bodily out of the window and beat him up in the street! When the other two went out he beat them up as well. Oliver might have been a little bloke but we all treated him with a little more respect after that. A lot of respect if he was moody.

This strange crowd invited me and John to the Hole in the Wall bar one night and we were amazed by the dolly birds that gathered around them. Maybe the girls thought they were safe. Maybe they weren't girls! Either way me and John played safe and kept our grubby little hands to ourselves, which was a first for John.

Chapter 11 More Rock

There was nothing quite like a long weekend in Gib, a weekend free from duties (and RPs!) and an excuse to escape from Lathbury. John Curry was now firmly established in the cookhouse and we would often disappear around the back end of the rock with crates of beer and a box full of steaks. I can't imagine where the steaks came from. If you are ever lucky enough to visit Gibraltar, pop round to the water catchment area. You'll find a huge cave there with relics like rusty beer cans and the odd fossilised squaddie. If we weren't doing that we would go on the town from Friday night until Monday morning, such were the opening hours. It was after one of those 'lost weekends' when I turned up on a Monday morning parade with the shakes. I wasn't happy about that so I laid off the beer that night. The RQMS, WOII Shave, took the parade on Tuesday morning and he came up to me. "Were you on the piss last night?" he asked, "You look like shit!" It was probably the only night in the last few weeks that I hadn't been on the beer and he thought I looked like shit?

Among the many duties carried out in the camp was 'Canteen Cowboy', a duty normally carried out by an NCO. For some strange reason they gave me this role. Perhaps they'd run out of NCOs or they thought it was funny. Either way it was nice to be entrusted with such a responsibility. All I had to do was keep an eye on the NAAFI and make sure the soldiers behaved themselves, after which I would lock down the NAAFI and Corporals Mess. Clearing the NAAFI wasn't a problem, they went away happy, but the Corporals Mess would be something else. How does a Private tell a Corporal it's last orders and time to go home? As luck would have it there wasn't many NCOs in there and I approached one who was just leaving. "Is that everyone out?" I asked him. He staggered against the door frame and peered at me. "Yep!" he said, "Unless you count Corporal Chinn." Then he teetered away. Not Corporal Chinn! I knew the 'Chinn' but I'd never really spoken to him, he usually passed people in the camp and growled at them. He was one of the Battalion's old sweats and had seen action in Aden. I can only describe him as the original hard man. So my heart sank when I heard he was still in the Corporals Mess. I slowly moved into the darkness of the bar and I could just make out the shape of a body on the pool table, a body that was clearly fast asleep. I looked at the motionless Chinn and decided I had two options available to me. I could wake him up and risk certain death or I could leave him there for the cleaners in the morning. I decided he probably wouldn't kill a cleaner so I locked up leaving him on the pool table.

The Chinn

One weekend Andy Hawker and I decided to do something different with our Saturday morning and we paddled a dinghy out to sea. We sat crossed legged in our rubber craft and just paddled our cares away. After a few hours we started to head back but the tide had turned and we had a battle on our hands, either we would get back to Gib or end up in Morocco. We did make it back but, with all that sitting crossed legged under the sun, my knees were knackered and looked like swollen footballs! On the Monday morning I could barely get my trousers past my swollen joints so I went off to the medical centre walking like Douglas Bader. The MO diagnosed water on the knee, or housemaid's knee, and put me on light duties. We had a cross country run coming up soon and it looked like I wouldn't be playing a part in that. But this is the Army and you don't get off that easy, so it was decided that I would be one of the marshals on the route. The day of the run came and I struggled down to where the marshals were forming up. "Where's your fackin' belt!?" the NCO in charge yelled at me. Rats! In my struggle to get my trousers on and the thought of negotiating 4 flights of stairs, I'd forgotten my belt. "Double away and get it!" he screeched. Having a laugh wasn't he? Now I had to struggle up those stairs again, get my belt and struggle back. This took some effort and by the time I got back they had all left. No doubt I'll be in the shit again. "Quick march!!" yelled the Sergeant Major knowing full well that my legs were stuck in waddle mode. I shuffled in and stopped at Major Waite's desk. He looked up at me with a quizzical eye, possibly the glass one. "Something wrong with your legs?" he asked. "Housemaids knee!" said Noddy before I could say water on the knee. I detected a look on the Major's face that said 'That'll stop the little bugger kicking my desk.' I was summarily charged and given the usual 7 days RPs then the Sergeant Major shuffled me out. Oh well, I least I couldn't drill on the show parade...

There was something stirring about listening to the bugler play the last post when I was on show parade, but one night it didn't go quite as it should have done. We all stood on parade and the Duty Officer and the Battalion Orderly Sergeant arrived. "Duty bugler!" ordered the BOS, "Sound the last post!" The bugler placed the instrument to his lips and blew. Exactly what he blew I wasn't sure but it certainly didn't sound like the last post. It sounded more like a cat trapped in a tumble drier, it was awful. We all had a discreet glance in his direction expecting to see him dressed in a clown's outfit, but he wasn't. The Duty Officer and the BOS stood motionless, saluting as the flag came down. At the end of it they both dropped their saluting and the Duty Officer was the first to speak. "Battalion Orderly Sergeant!" he bellowed. "Yes Sir?!" the BOS replied. "Lock up the duty bugler!" Mick Talbot, the bugler, was marched into the guardroom and spent the next 2 hours running about with a concrete filled artillery shell. But at least it took the heat off me that night. The next morning Mick was marched into Dickie Waite's office and got 5 days RPs. 5 days? Dickie must have liked him.

Those seven days seemed to drag by but they did come to an end so a few of us decided to disappear round the rock for the weekend. Crates of beer were collected from the NAAFI and steaks were, well, 'obtained' from somewhere or other. We left the barracks and headed off past the

WWII gun emplacements when we spotted a familiar figure sitting by a dwindling fire. It was the Chinn. Maybe if we quietly crept behind him he wouldn't notice us and we wouldn't disturb him. No such luck, he probably smelled the steaks or the beer. Rather than bark and growl at us, he invited us over to where he was sat. I could see something unrecognisable in the ashes of his smouldering fire. "Where are you lot off to?" he asked. We told him we were just on an excursion to the water catchment area. We sat with Bob Chinn and shared his 'fire' while he shared our beer and a steak. He was a very profound person and told us how he was soon to leave the Army, move down south and get himself a fishing boat. It would be a sad day when Bob left, he was one of the well-established characters in the Battalion. No longer would we hear an officer asking "Where's the Chinn?" or "Have you seen the Chinn about?" He did eventually leave the Army but I'll never know if he ever got his boat. I did know that he was irreplaceable. Some people would try to emulate this legend but came nowhere near. Anybody who knew Bob would tell you that he was a one off and is probably worth a book all of his own. Having had a fascinating conversation with the Chinn, we continued to our cave where stories of Bob were the main topic...

Fred Tubeless from the imagination
of Capt. Christmas

But we still had other characters with us, characters like 'Niff'. For years I only knew him as Niff, even the officers called him Niff! It's only thanks to friends on Facebook that I now remember his name as Lancaster. But he was a popular bloke and everyone seemed to know him. Another one of our well known personalities was an officer, Captain Christmas. I first got to know him because he had a slot on BFBS radio (British Forces Broadcasting Service). Once a week we would listen in for 'A letter home from Private Fred Tubeless', Fred being the alter ego of Captain Christmas. Being a cartoonist I had my own idea of what Fred Tubeless looked like and made a sketch of him. I presented it to the Captain and hoped that it didn't offend him. I needn't have worried. "That's him!" he exclaimed with excitement and he was very happy that Fred had finally got a face to go to his character.

Probably my finest achievement in Gibraltar was painting the Battalion Colours board and the Queen's Colours board. The originals were works of art and were painted by my predecessor Garry Sutcliffe. But they were beginning to look a little faded and wrinkled, so I was tasked with reproducing them. It took months to do and, although I was proud of them, they weren't a patch on the originals. But they were good and were mounted on the walls of the HQ building. (Not only had I done something rather special but it got me off a lot of parades too!) My reward for these works of art was the highest honour that the Commanding Officer could bestow upon me: the presentation of a Regimental Recognition Tie! Don't laugh, not everybody got one. So it made a change to stand outside any commander's office and not be in trouble. Then the RSM informed me that my moment of glory would be delayed, they were waiting for a prisoner; a prisoner who was guilty of heinous crimes that were contrary to the good name of the Battalion. It wasn't long before I heard the 'Left! Right! Left! Right!' of a prisoner being double marched from the far end of the corridor. Although I was stood to attention I couldn't resist a peek at the approaching villain. The skinny figure looked a sorry sight, his pockets hung out and his shirt tail billowing in his wake. There was a torn breast pocket and a cigarette drooping from his lips. Cigarette? Drooping from his lips?! As the sorry creature drew closer I could see it was Captain Christmas in the guise of Fred Tubeless. He was marched into the COs office where the charges were very loudly read and, after a few minutes, he emerged clutching his Regimental Recognition Tie. Laugh, I nearly wet myself on parade. The presentation of my tie wasn't so entertaining but at least I was in good company. And yes, I've still got it.

Captain Newman was still his eccentric self and his good friend Captain Pace was due to leave us in the next week or so. Captain Pace once confided in him that he once had a nightmare where the QM had painted an orange stripe down the rock face of Gib. (The orange stripe was something that Captain Newman insisted was incorporated on all of our Battalion sign boards.) Well that sowed a seed in the mind of our good Captain and he came down to the workshop. He took Barry and a few others to one side and told them he wanted an orange stripe down the rock face when Captain Pace was departing at the airport. He would achieve this by having Barry and co. hiding in a cave and tossing out a mile of orange bunting! With the face of the rock facing the airport everyone would see the glory of it all. Being the QM he had no problem ordering huge swathes of bunting and, being the QM, he had no problem coercing Barry and the others in carrying out his plan. On the day of his departure Captain Pace and his entourage left the airport building and made their way to the aircraft. Captain Newman gave the signal and this huge piece of cloth was hurled from its hiding place, unfurling itself into an orange stripe. Alas, the face of the rock is a gigantic mass and the acres of bunting looked no more than a piece of loose cotton thread. Captain Pace eventually saw it, after lots of pointing and some squint eyed peering. It would seem that even the mighty Captain Newman couldn't upstage the rock!

There's more to Gibraltar than meets the eye, it's more than just a lump of rock. Most people will be familiar with areas in the rock, like the upper St. Michael's Cave where they have displays. Our own band often held concerts in there. But go a little deeper and you have the lower St. Michael's Cave which is more primitive in its surroundings. Normally John Curry and I would never have seen this but it just so happened that a certain barmaid, who played the Jews Harp, had an engineer husband who was a guide there. So one day we went down into the bowels of the rock with our engineer friend leading the way. What a place! There were no coloured lights here like in the upper caves, only a string of naked light bulbs. To navigate this giant pothole involved clambering about on ropes, which made me glad John Gibbs wasn't there. It was certainly a hazardous place but there were a lot of things to be seen. Like the stalagmite that resembled Winston Churchill, another that looked like a mother and baby and one that took the shape of a barbary ape. But the highlight of the tour was the underground lake, a lake of undefinable depth at the time and nobody knew where it led to. We viewed this from a thin ledge that ran around its edge and our guide informed us that the ledge was formed by millions of years of dust. So we all shuffled along it and were happy to be back on terra firma. But it was truly amazing, one of those experiences that would live with me forever.

One day I nipped off to have my teeth looked at, although some would cruelly say it was my head which needed looking at. They could be right but, for now, I'll settle for my teeth. I'm glad to say that my Austrian friend from Cyprus wasn't there. After a quick inspection it was decided that they were fine and only needed a scale and polish. "Fine," I thought, "I'll have my teeth pampered" (except for the one I left in Cyprus). I sat in the dentist's chair and ogled the voluptuous young dental hygienist who would be molesting my molars. She was certainly pretty, something you don't often see in the barracks. While I sat there she almost straddled me and poked about in my mouth, a pleasant experience which required me to sit with my hands in my lap. "Just turn your head to the right," she instructed. I did and found myself with a soft boob stuck in my eye which caused me to slobber over her stainless steel instruments. Nothing came of this cheap thrill except I had to limp back to barracks.

A few weeks leave came my way and I decided to fly home to see family and friends. It was an enjoyable two weeks and during that time there was a mix up with the Services Booking Centre, nobody seemed sure when my flight was. So I missed it and was officially declared AWOL. I had to do something so I took a walk to the local police station and explained my predicament to them. They kindly gave me a travel warrant to Bassingbourn and told me I would have to sort it out there. So I caught the train to Royston and within a few hours I was walking into the guardroom. I introduced myself and explained the situation. "You're bleedin' AWOL!" said the Corporal, and then he locked me up in a cell.

Well, I'd been locked up before but never in my own civilian clothes. But the Provost staff were an obliging bunch and managed to scrounge a pullover and a pair of fatigue trousers from somewhere.

On my first morning there, I was marched off to the cookhouse with the other prisoners for breakfast. We all walked in the cookhouse, flicked the lights on and watched the cockroaches run for cover. I wondered if these were the same cockroaches that we had years before or whether they were a new generation following in their parents' footsteps. Then we were all marched back again. During the day there was very little to do, a walk around the exercise yard and the occasional smoke in the guardroom. To keep us occupied they would have us mopping out the cells and making the brass fittings nice and shiny. One night, the Duty Officer made his rounds and decided to inspect our cells. I stood to attention at my cell door and he brushed past me only to return holding a dusty forefinger in my face. "Do you see that?" he asked, waving the digit before my eyes. Surely it wasn't my job to clean the officer's finger was it? "Yes Sir!" I said. "It's dust!" he informed me. If he was waiting for some sort of reply it was going to be a long night. "It's your dust!" he yelled. "And to prove it's your dust look..." he then proceeded to rub the dust onto the pullover I was wearing. "See!" he shouted triumphantly, "It came off on your pullover!" Because I'm a nice bloke, I didn't have the heart to tell him it wasn't my pullover. It was obvious that he was in a bad mood and after glancing round the guardroom he spotted a brass valve about twelve feet up the wall. He wasn't happy about the state of it and demanded that we prisoners should get it gleaming by the time he returned later. I climbed onto someone's shoulders but I couldn't reach it, so he got on a chair with me on his shoulders and we managed at a stretch. Where on earth was Health and Safety in those days? The duty Rupert was as good as his promise and returned. He studied the brass valve then left, not even a thank you.

After a fortnight enjoying the hospitality of the Provost Staff I was transported to Brize Norton where I had a flight booked. The Provost Corporal handed me over to the duty snowdrop who locked me up until my flight the next morning. I was somewhat surprised the following morning when I saw one of our own Provost Staff come through the cell door, Corporal Martin Mills, in civvies. Apparently he was coming off his leave and volunteered to escort the prisoner on the aircraft. We walked out across the tarmac with Corporal Mills gripping my arm; did he really think I was going to make a run for the perimeter fence? Once we were seated on the aircraft I thought a little polite conversation would pass the time. "How are you Corporal Mills?" I asked. "Be quiet!" he snapped. "OK then." "Shut it!" "Alright." "I won't tell you again!!" All in all, it was probably the most boring flight of my life and I only had the sick bag to read. When the plane did land at Gibraltar, Corporal Mills was the first to stand up. "Please remain seated while I remove this prisoner!" he shouted down the length of the aircraft. The rest of the passengers must have thought he'd caught one of the Kray twins. Soon I was stood before Dickie Waite's desk once again, nice to see a familiar and friendly face. After the usual pleasantries and looking for his glass eye I marched out with RPs. Guess how many?

One night, some of us had a chance to skip off the usual chores when we were offered the chance of 'volunteering' as waiters for an Officers Mess dinner. It sounded like a good deal to me, I'd done something similar before and we waiters did have a few beers at the end of the night. When the meal was finished and the officers had left we cleared everything away then put our feet up with a few beers. We were chatting away when Captain Newman appeared in the doorway. "Sorry lads," he said looking around the room, "but my wife left her scarf behind." "Where is she Sir?" we asked. "Oh, she's waiting in the car. If I can just find her scarf..." "Bring her in Sir," we implored, "you can both have a drink with us." This wasn't the Captain's thing at all but, after some deliberation, he surprised us all and agreed. "I don't suppose one would hurt," he said and went out to fetch Mrs Newman. She plonked herself next to me and was very down to earth, nothing like the Captain. "So how come you're waiting on this lot then?" she asked. I told her that I was AWOL and now I was serving my penance. "Ooh," she said, "I remember Peter doing that!" She leaned across me and spoke to Captain Newman. "Remember that Peter? Remember when you were AWOL? Peter?" The Captain didn't want to hear or remember. What an eye opener that was! But we had a laugh and eventually found her scarf. That, unfortunately, was the only time I met her but I would be learning more about the Captain very soon...

A contingent of the Battalion would be going to Kenya on an exercise and this meant some of HQ Company and the QMs department. Surely they would need a signwriter? I marched into his office, threw up a smart salute and pleaded my case. "See that picture on the wall behind you?" he said without looking up from his paperwork. I turned and looked and, yes, there was a picture there, only a small one in a frame but a picture all the same. "Yes Sir." I replied, puzzled. "Take it down," he told me, "and read the back of it." I did as I was ordered and there, stuck to the back, was a citation typed on yellowed paper. I can't remember it word for word but it concerned 'Sergeant Newman' and his actions some thirty-odd years ago. He was in a trench when the Mau Mau attacked his position and he had no rounds left. With the attackers almost upon him he fixed his bayonet and sprang from his trench. Luckily for him the Mau Mau were using homemade weapons which failed to fire so he managed to bayonet the three of them to death. I finished reading the enlightening report and turned to the Captain. "And the problem is, Sir?" I asked naively. He looked up from his paperwork and fixed me with a bayonet wielding gaze. "The problem is," he said, "that took place in Kenya and one of the attackers was a Mau Mau Prince. I can't go to Kenya and neither can you." Then he went back to his paperwork, end of discussion. Because of something he did over thirty years ago meant I couldn't go to Kenya and that was that. Cheers Cap'n.

All in all the Battalion had spent two years on the rock, some said that was too long but I disagreed and said it wasn't long enough. Even though I became fondly known as the RP king, I enjoyed the tour tremendously and I'm certain there were more secrets hidden within the rock. But the Battalion was preparing for the move back to the UK and we, in the workshop, had thousands of crates to make to ensure that the families got their fridges and washing machines back safely. During a lull in the crate making I popped out for a smoke where I came across some members of the Peanut Platoon (Assault Pioneers). I don't remember how the banter went but they clearly took exception to one of my remarks and bundled me into one of our crates and nailed the lid on. Then I espied one of our officers heading our way. "Quick!" I told them, "Major White's coming! I can't salute him from inside a crate!" The peanuts insisted that I could and upended the crate to facilitate this. "Morning Sir!" I called from the confines of my wooden strait jacket and threw up a cramped salute. "Morning," replied Major White and saluted as if he salutes crates every day of the week. That should have been the end of my ordeal but a military minibus came round the corner. "Where are you going mate?" asked the peanuts. "I'm off down the docks," the driver told them. They threw my crate into the back of the bus and instructed him to drop it off down at the aforementioned docks. The driver happily obliged regardless of my pleas. And no, he didn't give me a lift back. I had to drag my crate all the way up the hill back to Lathbury Barracks. Shortly after that traumatic experience we left the rock one last time and flew back to the UK. Our next exotic location would be Catterick Garrison with all the biting wind and rain it could muster. Now, where were all those that said that two years in Gibraltar was too long?

Chapter 12   Somme Lines and Musgrave Park

Somme Lines in Catterick was our new home and would remain so for the next couple of years. The garrison wasn't so bad, there were plenty of watering holes and those dreaded RPs seemed an age away. While in Somme I was introduced to a couple of REME blokes that were attached to us: Corporal Vince Pickup and Sergeant John Riley. Vince was from Wigan and introduced me to the joys of Mike Harding and Uncle Joe's mint balls. John Riley wasn't Irish, as his name suggests, he was Fijian and spoke with a northern accent! But he was a big rugby fan and knew all the bawdy songs so he took centre stage in the workshop at Christmas.

The nearest town to us was Richmond and it had numerous pubs which was probably why Vince and myself would frequent the place. One night we both drank our way through the pubs in the market square and decided to go further afield, so we made our way up the hill to The Holly Hill Inn. It wasn't too far out and we both had a few pints of Old Peculiar, a nice pint indeed. At the end of the night we calculated that, if we ran down the hill, we could get to the chip shop before it closed. Off we went, me running down the road while Vince raced down the pavement. It might sound stupid that I was running down the road but at least it stayed level when we hit the bridge that crossed the river. The pavement was a different story. That crossed the bridge then went into a series of steps; steps that Vince failed to notice in his haste. It was very surreal as I ran along with Vince sailing past me, treading air as he went, then crashing into a heap on the pavement. Not only was he in a very untidy heap but his spectacles exploded on impact. We did get to the chip shop, with Vince standing in the queue trying to look nonchalant while everyone else viewed him like he'd been brawling. But he survived the night and we managed to get back to camp. I recently checked our route on Google street view and those same steps are still there, but no sign of Vince's glasses though...

Something strange happened in Catterick; I transferred to the Peanut Platoon. Why? Well Bill Dixon transferred there as Pioneer Sergeant and they played with big boys toys like explosives and things. Or maybe it was because they made such a huge impact on me when they nailed me into a crate! No sooner had I joined them than we got wind of another

Northern Ireland tour. We would soon be off to Musgrave Park in Belfast and our role would involve house searches and vehicle searching at the HGV centre, so we all went off to Chatham in Kent to learn these new skills. After that we had a few weeks leave then came back ready for the move. It was going to be different to patrolling the streets but, like every time I crossed the sea to Belfast, it was a worrying time.

October 1975

Musgrave Park was another one of those cosy camps full of portakabins and all laid out in the grounds of Musgrave Park Hospital which I found reassuring. Bill Dixon decided that the platoon would be split into two groups, one would be based in Belfast to conduct the house searches while the other would be down in Long Kesh for the HGV vehicle searches. After two weeks we would switch round. My first fortnight was in Belfast and any searches carried out were intelligence led with people tipping us off as to where arms or explosives were hidden. Occupied houses were straightforward affairs but unoccupied properties were a different matter altogether. With people in a house, it was unlikely that you would come across a booby trap device but if it was unoccupied there could be anything in there waiting for you. Most of these searches were carried out in the early hours of the morning because Bill probably thought we were too ugly to be let out in daylight. One day, under the cover of darkness, we left Musgrave Park and went to search a flat. We had the Drums Platoon acting as a cordon and they patrolled outside while we went in. The problem with a block of flats, even in those small hours, is that they know as soon as you're in the building, let alone at the apartment door. So the first find of a weapon went to the Drum Major. As we entered the block, one of the occupants decided to part with his incriminating rifle and threw it out of a window, where it came down at the Drum Major's feet. Drum Major Chapman complained that if it was a few seconds later it would have hit him on the head! Apart from that one weapon, the search yielded nothing.

Another tip-off had us searching yet another dwelling but this one was a house. The householder wasn't too pleased about such an early wake-up call so he was more than a little grumpy as was the rest of the family. Terry Prosser was one of our team and, because he was one of the taller ones, it was decided that he and another tall bod would search the downstairs rooms and out-houses. Me and another short arse would do the bedrooms and attic. This was a fine plan except that me and my fellow short arse got delayed searching the bedrooms (something to do with the meticulous detailed inspection between the pages of a porn mag). So Terry and his mate made a start on the attic. While I was in the bedroom, having put away the artistic magazines, the householder came in with Nobby Clarke our section leader. "What about any damage?" he asked. Nobby assured him that our team were professionals and knew exactly what we were doing. He also told him that in the unlikely event of any damage caused, there were official forms to be filled out. At that point a leg came through the ceiling. We could hardly say that it wasn't one of ours because it wore combat trousers and had a big boot on the end. Not only that but it was making a desperate bid to retract itself and disappear back into the loft, probably hoping that if he did it quick enough no one would notice. "That's an unusual light fitting," I remarked, but the householder had already left the room, no doubt filling out forms.

"Nice light fitting. IKEA?"

After two weeks of annoying the neighbours we went off to Long Kesh to relieve the other section. We drove out of Musgrave Park in our distinctive makrolon covered Land Rover, distinctive because we had a blue step ladder on the side which sat on brackets. The makrolon, we were told, would give us some protection from small arms fire. The ladders would make us taller when we needed to be. Small arms fire was a little worrying where Bob Keen and myself were concerned because we were doing top cover whereby we had our heads out of the top, looking forwards and rearwards. Even as we left camp the cold and rain were freezing my digits off. This was in the good old days when we wore those horrible green woollen gloves, the ones that held the water and were about as much use as a papier-mâché helmet. I was still cursing those stupid gloves when we approached the traffic lights, they were in our favour and the driver turned right. Then I saw the headlights of a vehicle bearing down on us. "He'll never stop," I thought. And I was right; he caught us right in the side of our Land Rover which spun it round the junction. My rifle, attached to my wrist with the sling, slipped from my wet gloves, went round in an arc and hit Bob square in the back of the head. "Debus!!" yelled Bill from the front, fearing we were under attack. We all leapt off and took up all round defence positions. We were all in place but where had Bill got to? Shouldn't he be with us? It would appear that the impact of the crash caused our step ladder to slide forward across Bill's door and he couldn't open it. After hearing his pleas for help we released him; it was the humane thing to do. It turned out that the driver of the car wasn't a terrorist, he was just some bloke rushing home because he was on a promise. Once we were happy that nobody was hurt and there was no real damage to our vehicle we continued on our way.

Not only was Long Kesh home to prisoners housed in the notorious H Block but it also had a hangar which was the HGV search centre. The Royal Military Police would escort the lorries in, we would search them and then we would escort them to the back gate. That was our routine for the next two weeks. But there were perks... Eric Dennis was our driver and he didn't mind who escorted the vehicles out, even though it was his Land Rover and we didn't have driving licences. Bob Keen and myself would often leap into the vehicle and go driving off, I saw it as practice for whenever I got a driving lesson. After searching yet another lorry I jumped into the Land Rover and escorted it out. As usual I drove through the camp to get back to the hangar but, on this occasion, one of the camp guards leapt out in front of me. I stopped and he approached my window. "Who are you wiv mate?" he asked with his clipboard in hand. "3 Queen's, HGV search centre," I replied pointing at my cap badge. "Got your ID?" he asked, clipboard at the ready. I did but I didn't want him to know that; I've seen clipboards before and they could be dangerous in the wrong hands. "I haven't," I lied, "it's back with my kit." He strained his neck and looked into the cab. "This your vehicle?" he asked. "Yes," I said, lying again. Then he brought the clipboard into the aim. "What name is it?" "Lance Corporal Dennis," I told him, hoping he wouldn't notice the lack of a stripe on my sleeve. He ran his pen down a list of names. "OK," he said, "carry on then." There's nothing like living on the edge is there?

Our two weeks at Long Kesh was now at an end and, because it was my birthday, nobody was happier than me. There was no beer at the hangar but back at Musgrave you were allowed two cans (a few more than that if you were extra nice to the Choggy Wallah!) And, as a bonus, they were screening 'The Exorcist'. Before we left, we had one more lorry coming in. We'd make a quick job of this and shoot off. The wagon pulled in and we opened the rear doors to peek inside. It appeared we had a lorry full of cows. But not whole cows, just bits of them. Row upon row of bins full of heads and stomachs, all destined for the pie factory. Rather than delve into the bloodbath before us, we decided to follow the lorry to the pie factory and supervise the unloading which would be less messy. At its final destination we all watched it unload, heads, legs and bellies all spilling out in front of our eyes. After that The Exorcist was nothing.

We had one of those days in the camp at Musgrave where we were all at a loose end, we did a house search in the early hours and now we were twiddling our thumbs. Rather than do nothing I gathered some of our section by the side of our vehicle and held an impromptu briefing. With my finger I drew the outline of the plan on the dirty makrolon of the Land Rover and spouted claptrap. By the end of it I had drawn a three foot willy. We all laughed about it but Bill had a fit when he saw it. He wasn't amused and, after an ear bashing, ordered me to take the wagon down to the wash-down point and clean the filth off. I didn't know if 'filth' meant the dirt or my three foot willy but I washed it anyway. That afternoon I sat in my portakabin doodling away when one of the lads came in carrying a bottle of poteen. This was an illegal clear liquid drink produced by the locals. God only knows where he got it from, I only knew that it could blow the nuts off an elephant. He offered me a drink of this poison but I declined. Then he poured some into my paint tray and lit it. There was a flash and our eyebrows disappeared. After that demonstration I had a tot. Can you believe that? After drinking that, it wasn't my eyebrows I was worried about.

We couldn't sit around doing nothing all the time so, after another tip off, we went to search a building site. When we got there we found the gates padlocked but that was no problem for the bolt croppers we carried with us. We spent the morning searching everywhere that might yield a cache of explosives or a few rifles but there was nothing so we stopped and gathered our thoughts. We were considering our next course of action while standing by a freshly built brick wall, a wall about six feet high and twenty feet long. Bob Keen stood astride a trench that ran the length of the wall and, as we moved off, he used the brick structure for support to step over the trench. Everyone stood gob smacked as the huge wall folded and twisted until it was flat on the ground. So now we knew what we would do next, retreat back to camp! Bob said it wasn't a very good wall anyway, and he should know, he was a bricky.

Shortly after that episode we were called upon to search another occupied house. After gaining entry, the family were placed in the front room while we went about our business of poking our noses into theirs. There was nothing to be found here either so, after doing my bit of searching, I started to put the towels and bed linen back into the airing cupboard. At that point the householder's son came and gave me a hand. "What a good lad," I thought. Then the RUC came in and arrested him on suspicion of armed robbery. That was a surprise, but not as big as the surprise I got when I stepped out of the front door. The Land Rover stood at the kerbside with the early morning sun shining off its side panel and the thing that caught everyone's attention was the three foot willy. Oh bugger! I'd obviously marked the surface of the IR paint and now my willy had come back to haunt me. I stood to attention in front of Captain

Newman, QM and acting OC. He made it very plain that he wasn't impressed with my artistic endeavours. "I'm just glad it wasn't going around Belfast like that!" he yelled, but he didn't know that it had been all over Belfast like that for the last two weeks. After a dressing down he fined me £15. Not bad for a three foot willy, it worked out at £5 a foot. Needless to say, I had to paint the vehicle too.

Bill got the section together one afternoon and told us we would be going out in the early hours to search an unoccupied house. These were the stuff of nightmares because anything could be waiting for us in there. When we arrived there, the house stood all on its own in the middle of nowhere and looked very dark and menacing. First we had to clear the way to the front door, checking inch by inch as we went. This was a long drawn out job but it was necessary for the safety of us all. Then we had to slowly work our way through the house looking for anything out of place like wires, marzipan smells or signs of a recent visit. One of the pieces of equipment we carried with us was a box with a bulb, battery and an alarm clock. It looked every bit like a bomb and we used it to shine a light up the chimney (you wouldn't point your torch up there in case of light sensitive photo cells and a lump of semtex). The box would be set in the hearth, timer set for fifteen minutes and we would retreat to cover for thirty minutes. If nothing blew up, we could resume the search. Placing our 'light bomb' in the fire place fell to me. I crawled up to the fire place and started to set it up. Everything went fine until I connected the battery and the light bulb lit up! As luck would have it there was no bang and I had time to think "Holy shit!" But I didn't want to look like a tit so I set the timer properly, crept away to cover and waited the prescribed thirty minutes. We all sat behind a wall waiting for the possible bang. Well they were, I already knew there wouldn't be one! I'd made a basic mistake that could have cost me my life and I consider myself very lucky indeed. Next time I'll engage my brain.

There was another search where I literally took my life into my hands. The IRA decided to get rid of some of their mortar bombs so they fired them at one of our other locations in Belfast. Luckily they all missed and landed in the deserted yard of a 'bacon factory'. However they didn't all explode which meant that we were called in to find the unexploded ones. The yard was a large area covered in weeds and scattered bushes so we made a start point and systematically worked our way through, leaving no stone unturned. I came across one of the small bushes and peered beneath it where I saw, what appeared to be, some red and silver foil. So I moved it. Now I don't know about you but I would have expected a mortar bomb to be green and brown, much like our own really. But no, their mortars were red and silver and looked a lot like the one in my hand. I called Bill Dixon over and he inspected the object with its sweaty explosive hanging out. "Just place it on the ground," he said. When I'd done that he beat me on the helmet. "What did you pick it up for, you stupid twat!?" Good question but I didn't have much of an answer ready.

There were times when we had to play our part in guarding the hospital, obviously with the Army camped in its back garden it was always going to be a target. I was on the reception desk one evening when all hell broke loose, a helicopter was about to arrive from South Armagh carrying injured soldiers. They were injured during a fire fight in Forkhill and it didn't sound good. There was nothing we on the guard could do, it was all down to the medical staff. The helicopter arrived and the first soldier stretchered through was suffering gunshot wounds and I'll always remember him screaming for his mum. The other two soldiers were carried through in silence. They were both dead. Suddenly I realised that soldiers often do make the ultimate sacrifice in times of trouble. Phone calls were made and grieving parents were flown out to Belfast. I'll remember that night for the rest of my life. Our six months in Belfast was at an end and we rolled out of camp and made our journey back to Catterick.

Chapter 13 Wedding Bells

Catterick hadn't changed, there were still fights between rival units and an abundance of beer to be drank. I didn't bother with the first but I did my level best with the latter. A great deal of beer was consumed at this time because I was soon to be wed to Pam and I was on a strict training programme with the help of a few friends! I sat in the NAAFI one night, on my own, and chatted to the barmaid. There was only the two of us so we had a nice natter. The NAAFI had a huge panoramic window which looked out onto the camp and that's when we both saw the barrel chested figure walking past. "Blimey," said the barmaid, "He looks a hard 'un." And he did. He walked into the bar and strode up to the counter, shoulders back and chest jutting out. "Half a lager and lime," he said in a most effeminate voice. The barmaid, finding it difficult not to laugh, said something about changing a barrel and she disappeared round the back of the bar where I could hear her guffawing. That was OK but I had to sit there with a straight face. That person was Chesty Morgan, a nice enough bloke and he would end up serving in my platoon. As for the barmaid, I'll never forgive her for that!

I was coming out of the NAAFI one night and happened to pass the Corporals Mess, a room next to our humble bar, and saw Pedro Ford and Jock Perry in there. These were two NCOs in the ACC (Army Catering Corps) and, having spent all day cooking, liked nothing more than having a few pints after work. When they saw me they beckoned me in. I was a bit wary because this wasn't my place but, after a quick look around to ensure there was nobody else in there, I went in. I took a seat at the bar and they got me a beer. I hadn't really met them before but we got on fine. I knew of Pedro, he got thrown out of the Colburn Lodge pub for playing the spoons, the gaffer said they didn't have a music licence. Jock was a hard Scotsman who liked his whisky. (Why do whisky drinkers pull such a face when they drink it?) He told me about being pulled over by the police when he was on his way home from the Mess. He was most upset because they banned him from riding his bike! They were lovely blokes and I was friends with them for life after that, even though I needed sub-titles where Jock was concerned.

The best thing about being in the Peanut Platoon was the ability to create big bangs so when the Battalion decided to have an open day, the CO came to us for a pyrotechnic display. Early in the day we posed with our equipment and explained to the public what we did. Then we sneaked off and planted a lot of 'puff bags' in the arena to simulate an artillery bombardment. The puff bags were cotton bags filled with gunpowder and set off using an ISFE electric match. One push of a button and we had a nice bang and a plume of smoke. The public seated themselves and a bunch of 'terrorists' came on and hid in camouflaged goalposts. Before they came under attack by the good guys they were softened up with our artillery attack, lots of smoke exploding all over the arena. It may not have worried our 'terrorists' but I think some of the spectators wished they had brought spare underwear. Helicopters flew the attacking forces in and the battle was fought and, of course, the good guys won. After that demonstration the Band and Drums marched on playing suitably victorious music. While that was happening I went round to see the lads, asking them how it went from their point of view. "One of mine didn't fire," Bob Keen said. "Which one was that?" I asked him. "This one," he told me as he touched the contact. The Drum Major didn't even look the slightest bit startled as the as the charge erupted in front of him, he must have had nerves of steel. I'd like to think that the audience didn't notice this slight glitch but, somehow, I think one or two might have seen it in the corner of their eye...

Most of that year was taken up by courses. I was either learning to build bridges, purifying water, laying mines, clearing mines, using explosives, watermanship training or tying knots. Most of this was done in Chatham, Kent. That wasn't a bad thing because my uncle lived down there and I spent many weekends with him, my auntie and my cousins. This, of course, involved a little drinking. Cheers uncle Stan.

When I was in Catterick there was always someone who wanted to go out on the beer so one night I chose to go out with Eric Dennis and his wife Kathy. With the wedding looming up I saw this as a safe bet and we ended up in a club to watch a drag show. (No, I wasn't the main attraction!) It should have been a relaxed affair but, as usual, I had far too many beers than was good for me and after half a dozen barrels of Yorkshire's finest ales I bumped into a girl who had a somewhat tarnished reputation. I'm sorry to say that I ended up back at her place. What a shock it was for me to wake up to her the next morning! (She might have thought the same thing but I'm writing this book and she isn't.) With the beer still sloshing around my head I made my excuses and left for barracks. No sooner had I arrived than Andy Hawker rolled up. "Where were you last night?" he asked. I gave him a rough idea where I was. "Who was she then?" he queried. At first I wouldn't say because I knew she was married to a soldier in our own Battalion, and I knew that he knew too. But in the end I told him. "You know she's got the clap don't you," he said. Well, these kindly words cut through me like a rusty bayonet. He also told me she was caught in some bloke's locker in one of the company lines one night, and it wasn't just the owner of the locker who enjoyed her charms!

Monday morning came and I sauntered off to the Medical Centre to confess and seek advice. I saw Alan Richardson, the medic, and told him my tale of woe. "Who was it?" he asked. I really didn't want to say but he told me who it probably was and he was right. "Oh dear," he said, making it obvious that he didn't share my taste in fallen women. Thinking about it she was probably more 'dropped' than fallen. He assured me that the story of her having the clap was false; it was put around to lure a soldier into coming forward. He then told me that the top brass were aware of her and would like to see the back of her. I told him that if the top brass bought her half a lager they could see more of her than just her back. But what they really needed was a soldier to confirm their worst fears then they could do something about her. I told Alan that I wanted no part of it but it didn't stop him ringing Major Dickie Waite. After a short chat on the phone, Alan turned to me. "The OC has guaranteed complete anonymity and says you'll only be referred to as 'a soldier'." That was fine for him to say, the Major had no idea who this 'soldier' was yet. I tapped on the OCs office door. "Come in!" he bellowed. I entered and threw up a salute and the poor Major nearly choked on his cup of tea. "You?!" he spluttered, "I've got to call you a soldier??" Never have I felt so sorry for a man holding the Queen's commission...

After that shabby incident I kept my tadger under lock and key. After all, my wedding day was only a few months away. My bride to be was Pam, a girl I met on leave in Coventry and I was about to pop home on leave to see her. We had such a wonderful time that I forgot to go back. Well, I didn't actually forget, I just decided to ignore it. I was AWOL yet again, not the first time but it would be the last. I was enjoying a lie in on this extended leave when two burly coppers came knocking on the door. Luckily my parents were at work so that spared them the embarrassment. So I 'went quietly' as the police would say. They put me in the police car and took me to Fletchamstead Highway police station where I was locked in a cell. It was only round the corner from where Pam lived on Centenary Road, if I could have seen through the glass block windows I would probably have seen her house. The Desk Sergeant paid me a visit and told me that my unit had been informed and they would be sending someone to pick me up. Aw shit, that could only mean Bomber Brown, another one of our Regimental Policemen, a rugby player and someone with a reputation of eating soldiers. Maybe I could hang myself with knotted toilet paper before he got here.

The Land Rover did turn up but it wasn't Bomber Brown. It was two lads from the platoon and a driver. Charlie Barber was one escort and Nobby Clark the other. The driver was Dennis Elvidge from the MT platoon and a Coventry lad. It didn't take me long to successfully plead with them to see Pam so we rolled up outside her house, got her on board and went to The Phantom Coach for a drink with her. (After all, Dickie Waite was still the OC and I might get life imprisonment.) As it happened any money I had was sealed in a plastic bag, courtesy of West Midlands Police, so Nobby paid for the beer. After a few drinks we dropped Pam off and went on another mission; we had to visit Dennis' mum and dad at the local TA Centre and fuel up the vehicle. At one point the beer got to my bladder and I had to slip off to the toilet and when I returned I told Nobby I could have slipped out of the loo window. "You wouldn't do that," said Nobby with confidence. "What makes you so sure?" I asked him. "You still had a pint on the bar" he said smiling. Very true, I'd never leave a pint. Because someone put the wrong fuel in the vehicle we had to stay with Mr and Mrs Elvidge that night until we got the tank flushed out. And very nice they were too.

We got back to Somme Lines the following evening where I was put in another cell until my audience with Dickie. Next morning I paid an escorted visited to Major Waite, looked for his glass eye and marched out with seven days RPs. It was good to be back. Nobby told me that, because they had to stay out overnight, they made a claim. I thought I'd try that. I went to the Pay Office and spoke to the Pay Corps Sergeant Major behind the desk. "You'll get fuck all!" was his reply, and it wasn't negotiable.

August 1976

At last, on the 7th August, I married Pam. John Bloom, the only mate I had left in Civvy Street, was my Best Man and Bill Dixon, Nobby Clarke and Vince Pickup came as guests. I would have got married in my drab Khaki No.2s but Captain Newman insisted that I should wear the very smart Blues uniform, complete with lanyard and white gloves. Because, as he put it, "I've never seen you look smart!" The wedding went fine and I returned to Catterick with Pam. We spent a few days living with Eric and Kathy Dennis while we waited for a married quarter then we moved into 54 Hambleton Road, a short walk from Somme Lines. Pam must have had an effect on me because I would never see those awful RPs again. I was a little concerned that being married would cramp my drinking habits. I worried needlessly; Pam would come with us and drink as much as the rest of us! After a few months of settling into married life, another posting cropped up: an unaccompanied posting to Belize.

Before I flew off to the Caribbean there were other things to do, like the Battle Fitness Test (BFT). This was usually a run on flat ground, outward bound together then the return as an individual effort, all timed of course. But some bright spark had the idea of making it more combat like. A ten mile forced march, with full kit, carry a man for ten yards, run to the 30 metre range and fire off five rounds. Is that all?? Off we went, looking like a long green centipede winding up the road. We would march some then run some. Then we would run some then march some. After ten miles of that we were paired off and had to carry each other the required ten yards. How I got paired off with Bob Keen I'll never know. There was me, a skinny bean pole and there was Bob, short and stout. He was clearly more knackered than me after the death march so I carried him first. It was agony, my legs grew more bowed with each step. But I made the ten yards and now it was my turn to take it easy. I climbed onto Bob's back and he collapsed in a heap. Bugger! After struggling through that caper we ran to the firing range, flopped onto the firing point and loaded a magazine of five rounds. I fired them off and had no idea if I hit the targets although I heard that two crows were strafed and a nun in Darlington received a 7.62 puncture in her rear bicycle tyre. There was a happy ending to this sorry tale, they decided to knock that silly idea on the head.

"C'mon John, I've a train to catch!"

With all of our kit packed it was time to say goodbye to Pam and make the migration to Belize. Pam, who fell pregnant while we were at home attending John Bloom's wedding, was disappointed. Our first born would arrive while I was away. But I had to go because I was a soldier. And it was warmer out there.

Chapter 14   Blue Skies and Belikin Beer

Belize wasn't just warmer, it was scorching hot. When the aircraft landed it didn't need to apply the brakes because the tyres melted on contact with the tarmac. Most of the landscape seemed to consist of jungle surrounded by jungle and Airport Camp, our new home, was just behind another strip of jungle. When you land in Belize you find a squadron of mosquitoes queuing up in the arrival lounge awaiting these 'whities from Blighty'. They liked nothing more than fresh white skin and within half an hour we looked like spotty teenagers. I shared the Belize experience with the old Peanut Platoon and Sergeant Bill Dixon was still very much in charge. There was also Corporal Reg 'Rags' Ryder, an older and stocky northerner who knew everything there was to know about knots and explosives. Want a knot tying? See Reg. Need something blowing up? See Reg. Need an exploding knot? Reg would probably sort that out too. Barry Morgan had joined us, old 'Chesty' from the NAAFI in Somme lines, a nice bloke but I always felt that he was more concerned about how he looked than what he was actually doing. He was great mates with Joe Frazier who was another one of our platoon. Bob Keen was still with us, now L/Cpl Keen, along with Jim Prior and Dave 'Borneo' Wildman. Dave really was an old sweat; he probably joined the Army when Centurion was a rank rather than a tank. Bill Dixon declared that this tour was to be his 'holiday'. "Because I deserve it," he said. We all agreed and felt much the same way so we decided to keep a low profile, only showing ourselves now and again to remind the Battalion we were still alive. We kept such a low profile that we could crawl under a closed door wearing a top hat.

Most of our days were taken up with sea fishing, boating, drinking and other military pursuits, a gruelling routine that was punctuated by work. It was during one of these rare work periods that I found myself digging out the concrete base of a defunct flagpole. It wasn't going too well and I was swinging the pick axe for all it was worth, aided by some colourful language which I thought would help. Then Bill came along. "Ah! Russell," he said, quiet and dignified. "What the fuck is it now!?" I said, not so quiet and definitely not very dignified at all. "The Adjutant is here to see you." I spun round and was stood face to face with Captain Harris. "Good morning Sir," I said, keeping a sweaty grip on my pick axe. "See me in my office at 11:00 hrs," said the Adjutant, then he walked off. I do wish people wouldn't creep up on me when I'm busy... At 10:55 hrs I was in my best O.G. shirt and shorts and stood outside the office. After all there's no point in looking sloppy when you get locked up is there? But I needn't have worried, the Captain just wanted to congratulate me on my promotion to L/Corporal. L/Cpl Russell. I liked the sound of that so much I'm going to write it again. L/Cpl Russell. Sigh.

"I hate sea fishing, I never get a bite."

After badly sewing the stripe onto my sleeve I went off to celebrate with Bill and Vince Pickup. First we went into the Handyside Bar, a favourite of ours, where we sank a few Belikin beers then moved onto Ma's. (Ma's was renowned for the best sizzling steak in Belize.) So we left the Handyside and made our way down the road, but Bill insisted we did it Northern Ireland style so we kept to the side of the roads and skirmished along. At this stage you need to know about the open sewage system in Belize City, a system of open drains that carried the waste and ultimately dumped it into the River. This is why they called it Sweet Water Canal. So there we were, bobbing and weaving down the road on route to Ma's steak house. I'm not sure if it was on the bob or the weave but my foot went into the roadside weeds and made a disgusting sludgy noise. Only Russell could step into the local sewer! Undeterred by this mortal wound to my foot we pressed on. We reached our destination and ordered three of those steaks that we knew would be sizzling on their iron plates when they arrived. While we waited we had a beer and Vince, rather foolishly, asked how my foot was. I raised it over the table and told him that the stench was wearing off a bit now. Fellow diners appeared to have lost their appetite over my offensive limb and left by the coachload which left us with the restaurant all to ourselves and the undivided attention of Ma.

"We hate to say it John, but it looks terminal."

We rounded the night off with a visit to the Hotel Continental, AKA the Big C. I'm not sure what the C stood for but I don't think it was continental. This was a lively, bustling place where BZ$20 would pay for the intimate company of a nice young lady, that's the sort of place it was. When we entered we spotted our friend Knacker at a table with his mates so we joined them. Knacker was a nice bloke but he was a little slow, so slow that someone had to look after his wallet for him when he went out otherwise he'd lose the lot. When we joined them Knacker's mates were egging him on to lose his cherry with one of the many girls available. "Go on Knacker," they insisted, "fill your boots! We'll even pay the twenty dollars!" Knacker spent an awful long time pondering over this and he eventually agreed. Off he went, led away by one of the young ladies. I personally thought this would be the death of him; this was new territory for our Knacker. We were still drinking and taking the piss out of anyone who warranted it when a grinning Knacker returned. "How did it go?" asked his mate. "I didn't do nuffin' did I," said the grinning Knacker, "we just talked didn't we!" All of our eyebrows shot off our foreheads. "That was a waste of twenty dollars!" I said. "Yeah," said Knacker, "I'm glad I didn't pay for it!" It was a joy to see Knacker laugh so much, but that was short lived when his mate pulled Knacker's own wallet out of his back pocket. "But you did pay for it!" said his mate, gleefully. Good old Knacker, a legend in his own lunch time.

I can't talk of the Big C without mentioning the toilets there. Not really a toilet, it was more of a pit, somewhere to make your bladder gladder. This foul swamp was probably the Sweet Water Canal estuary. It so happened that one of our Battalion fell into it one night and to say he wasn't a pleasant sight would have been an understatement. Not only did he look disgusting but he smelled terrible too. He was so bad that it took his mates all night before they could convince a taxi driver to take them back to camp. And then he only did it because he charged them BZ$30 for the BZ$5 trip! So it's true, when you're in the shit you soon know who your mates are.

One of the drivers at Airport Camp took 'going native' to a new level. He seemed to have ditched his uniform in favour of a pair of shorts and his hair grew beyond the limit of any decent soldier. I'll never know how he managed to maintain this new look because he was constantly driving around the camp in an open top Land Rover. He did this for months until an inquisitive officer asked an NCO who this 'civvy attached fellow' was. When the NCO told him that he was one of our soldiers, the officer almost died. After that, the soldier concerned had a haircut and wore half a uniform. But he enjoyed it while it lasted. It saddens me that I can't remember his name, but if I recall it I'll come back here and edit it!

Just off the coast of Belize was Ambergris Caye, a small strip of an island that was home to San Pedro, a one horse town with no horse. This was an R&R destination for some of the soldiers, somewhere they could go and get away from all that alcohol, and drink beer! The accommodation was a small lodge, a clapboard building rented by the Army. There was nothing at the lodge to speak of so you would take your sleeping bag and a ration pack. Sometimes the odd repair was required, so Bill would send me out there. On one occasion I had to fix a step so I went to the airfield, boarded a chopper with Crab Air and thirty miles later I was in San Pedro. That was on a Friday and there wouldn't be a return flight until the following Friday! Seven days to mend a step. Better than seven days RPs though. The step was duly repaired before the evening and the rest of my time was spent as a beach bum during the day and hovering between bars in the evening. Life was terribly hard sometimes.

The Army also owned a sailing boat at San Pedro which was looked after by one of the locals. I can't remember his name but he was a jolly man and a pleasure to spend time with. Someone thought that the boat needed a name so Bill sent me out there to do the signwriting on it and the boat would be called 'Guerro' or something similar. Vince Pickup came along for the ride; didn't the REME ever miss him? For me it was always the helicopter flight out there, the pilot would home in on the island then fly out to sea, swinging the aircraft side on. With the doors of the Puma open we could only see a wall of sea water flashing by our door with the centrifugal force holding us in our seats. A beautiful sight. We spent the Friday unpacking our tooth brushes then had a few beers that night. Then it was the weekend so we put our feet up and had a few beers. When Monday came I felt obliged to do some work so Vince and I waded out to the boat and I did my bit of signwriting. Because the boat wasn't going anywhere we sat on it with hand lines over the side but, not being a real fisherman, I just lazed there hoping not to get a bite. Then Vince had a brainwave. "Why don't you drop over the side," he said, "and find where the fish are?" That was a reasonable request so I donned the mask and snorkel and dropped over the side. (I said earlier in this book that I wasn't much for swimming but, in Belize and the Caribbean, you just have to!) Unlike that chlorine-filled pool in Bassingbourn, this was fresh, and wonderful. The clarity and the colour in the water were amazing because we were thirty miles from the Belize coast - otherwise it would be a murky brown and you would be dodging turds. It was so clear I could see the four foot barracuda that sat in the underwater vegetation fifteen feet away and swivelling its eye in my direction. It quickly occurred to me that this marine menace could see me too! I came out of the water like a Polaris missile, bounced on the deck of the boat and told Vince what I had seen. "Where was it?" he asked. "Over there!" I said pointing to the direction of the big fish. Rather than take my word for it Vince threw his hand line out towards the direction I gave him. Was he mad? I told him if that thing came aboard the boat I was off! That night we met an American marine biologist in one of the bars and she assured us that the barracuda didn't attack people although they have been known to nip at the soles of their feet because they look like small fish. I'll take her word for it.

Back at Airport Camp, Bill told us that we were to go down to Sibun, the jungle training camp. That was a little disconcerting, the Peanut Platoon playing soldiers!? Not at all, we were going there to clear an area in the jungle for a helicopter landing site which would involve lots of explosives. OK, I can live with that. Sibun was a training camp south of Airport Camp and sat alongside the Sibun River. No imagination spared there then. We rolled out of Airport Camp in our Land Rover with explosives and detonators bouncing about along with Vince Pickup. Did the REME ever hold a roll call? Our vehicle bounced along the dusty Western Highway heading south and, because we had to stretch our legs and save our fillings, we stopped at a roadside coffee bar. We dusted ourselves off and walked up to the café where we noticed a small monkey chained to a tree. None of us could resist his furry little charms and patted him on the head as we went by, such a friendly little primate. That was until Vince approached him, it didn't like him at all and it went mad. We could only assume that someone with a Wigan accent abused the poor creature or maybe it thought they were related.

The dusty Land Rover and its dusty occupants eventually arrived at Sibun Camp where Sergeant Major Jenkinson and Corporal Jim Laker met us. Did I say camp? There were three wooden sheds and a washing line surrounded by green jungle. I suppose you could call it minimalistic. Jim welcomed us and asked for a favour; could we blow a clearing in the nearby shrubbery so that they could demonstrate basher building to the troops? Of course we could, you can do almost anything with plastic explosives. PE4 was the choice of the Army and we used 80 lb, broken down into 4 oz charges, and spread it all about. We wired it all up, retired to a safe distance then pressed the button. There was a satisfying bang followed by smoke and vaporised jungle. The clearing they craved for was there for all to see, job well done. Well, we thought it was but Geoff Kilgarrif, Sibun medic, took a different point of view. "Look at this!!" he yelled poking his head out of a small shed. Apparently this small shed doubled as the kitchen and the medical centre and we sauntered over to him. "Look!" he squealed inviting us to cast an eye in there. The place was a mess with broken glass on the floor and all sorts all over the place. "You should keep all that stuff on the shelves," someone remarked. "It was on the pissin' shelves!" he shouted angrily, "Then you bleeders blew it all off!" That's a shock wave for you.

Favour number two. Jim said he wanted to build a shower and he needed the top lopping off a steel box. Jim had gone through a lot of trouble getting hold of this box and it was central to his shower plan. Well we could certainly help out there and got some det cord off the wagon. This looked like washing line and exploded with the help of a detonator. We unravelled it and wrapped it several times around the top of Jim's treasured box. The plan was that, on detonation, the top of the box would cut clean off. Again we retreated to a safe place to watch this spectacle. Except Geoff, he was busy sweeping up glass. The button was pressed and a loud bang ensued and was accompanied by a cloud of smoke which enveloped the box. The smoke drifted away and revealed a mangled lump of steel. Not quite what we had planned but hey ho.

As the training staff shelved their plans for a shower we gathered our kit and trudged off into the jungle where Geoff Kilgarrif enthusiastically waved us off. How he would miss us over the next few days. Our destination was a peak which we could see from the camp, its crown poking through the jungle canopy. It didn't seem too far away but it took us a whole day of hacking and climbing to get there. All of that hacking at foliage and splashing through streams must have been great for the eco system. On our arrival we began to build our A frames, a structure of sturdy branches, string and a poncho enabling us to sleep off the ground. That was a good idea because you didn't want to share your bed with a tarantula or Fleur-de-Lys snake. This had to be done fairly rapidly because we were losing daylight and when night fell in the jungle it seemed like the darkest place on earth. Lo and behold the daylight disappeared and so did everything else, it was like being blind. Because we were semi-tactical there were no lights or fires so we just slept and hoped the string would hold our A frames up until daylight. Next morning reveille was sounded by Bill blasting his Magnum pistol off. Yes, it was a bit over the top, but very effective. Bill loved his pistols and while he had his Magnum I carried his 9mm Browning and Vince was the custodian of the self-dismantling shotgun. This was an old weapon passed from one unit to another over the years and fell apart every time you fired it. But it was handy for shooting branches off trees before we felled them. After breakfast from our ration packs, we gathered on the peak. Bill had decided that a landing site would be too problematic so we would have to settle for a winch site. That way nobody would be cheated out of their fun and we still had trees to blow up. Bill laid down the ground rules, if explosives were about to be detonated he would give a blast on his whistle. That was it. That was the ground rule.

We clambered down the south side of the slope and selected our first tree. A hole was bored into the trunk, packed the PE4 in and placed the detonator. We then scarfed the safety fuse, lit it and walked back up the slope. (You never ran from a set charge. Not only does it look sissy but you might trip and roll back onto the explosive! Not recommended in any manuals I know of.) Bill blew his whistle and we waited for the bang. The explosion reverberated through the jungle and we went to inspect the fallen tree, except that it hadn't fallen at all. It just hung there, dangling in the air. We looked up and realised that the canopy of surrounding trees was holding it up. No problem, we would just blow the next tree. After more boring, more explosive and another whistle blast, we had another bang. Now we had two trees hanging there. We blew a third, then a fourth but they still hung there in defiance. Six trees later we stopped and pondered the problem over lunch. It was Dave 'Borneo' Wildman that came up with an inventive solution to the problem. He gathered some branches, strapped them together to form a frame and attached a charge to it. From the top of the peak he would light the fuse and toss the contraption onto the top of the canopy thus destroying the top cover and bringing the trees down. Sheer genius. We all gathered on the ridge to witness this spectacle. Dave produced his apparatus, lit the fuse and then, with a graceful, ballet like motion, he tossed it onto the canopy. We all watched in amazement as the frame landed on the foliage, fell through and bounced on the floor. The charge exploded creating a cloud of dust and the trees continued their mocking. Was Dave bothered by this failure? No, he just burst out laughing.

Don't you just hate it when that happens?

We would return to that problem later, meanwhile Vince and I went down the North slope to pick off a tree there. We had a little rain and the slope became somewhat slippery but we wouldn't be put off by nature's little quirks. While we bored a hole in the trunk and packed the explosive, the drizzle continued and the slope became a muddy river. We lit the fuse and paddled our way through the tide of slush but, as we neared the top of the ridge, I smelled burning safety fuse coming from ahead. I looked at Vince and Vince looked at me. "It's probably Bill burning off some off cuts," Vince suggested. He was probably right. After all Bill hadn't blown his whistle. We reached the top of the slimy ridge and my eyeballs popped from the comfort of their sockets, there in front of us was a lump of explosive stuck in a tree with its fuse burning away merrily! We went face down in the mud and the tree exploded whereupon it fell between us. The two of us climbed onto the ridge looking like shit monsters, neither of us very happy. "For fucks sake Bill,"

I said, "what happened to the whistle blast?" Bill stood there calmly preparing another length of safety fuse. "No point," he said, "nobody took any notice anyway." Well, what can you say to that?

When nightfall came, we were tucked up in our bashers staring at blackness where we could hear the hanging trees laughing at us. I was curled up with the 9mm Browning while Vince snuggled up to his self-dismantling shotgun. At some point during the night we had a visitor. We couldn't see what it was but we knew that there were all sorts of creatures roaming about in the jungle. It could have been a jaguar or a tarantula with boots on, either way it was large and scavenging about between Vince's basher and mine. "Can you hear that, John?" asked Vince in a hoarse whisper. "Yes," I replied, "hopefully it'll bugger off." Then I heard Vince fumbling about in the dark. "I've got the shotgun trained on it!" he said, "I'll shoot it!" "Piss off!" I said with some urgency, "You'll blow me clean off the ridge!" "Keep still while I fire." That was it; I pulled out the Browning and pointed it in Vince's direction. "Fire that and I'll fire this!" I told him. It seems we had a Mexican standoff without the Mexican. The creature at the centre of this saga sauntered off down the slope and we would never know what it was. Was Vince's gun loaded? Mine was. Meanwhile the hanging trees stopped their laughing and crumpled to the jungle floor. Now we laughed, and when daylight came we would point at them and mock them without mercy.

Morning came and Bill's morning Magnum shattered the silence. He really should think about reviewing his reveille because when he fired the round, it took a chunk of tree out just below his supporting string that held his basher up. Yes, I agree, it would have made a funnier story if he had hit the string! After breakfast it was time to clear away the logs and leaves that resulted from the previous night's collapse and we blew a few more trees. After doing that it was too late in the day to journey back to Sibun so we spent another night sleeping in the blackness of the jungle. Without incident, I hasten to add.

In the morning we packed our gear, made our way back to the camp and arrived by lunchtime where we all stripped off and waded into the river for a bath. (For some odd reason they didn't have a shower.) Chesty Morgan quickly found that the millions of micro fish that populated the waters were attracted to the soap. So, without further ado, he leapt out, lathered soap suds around his nuts and went back in. Ecstasy was written all over his face. Lucky for him there were no piranhas in these parts otherwise he wouldn't have had a face to write anything on. Then we climbed out and picked up our clothes that had been worn for the last few days - Phwoar! The smell could have brought a tear to the eye of a needle! Our kit stunk of dead vegetation which you didn't really notice as it crept over you. We had dinner then set off for Airport Camp, to a world of bed sheets and toilets. I can't be certain but I'm sure Geoff Kilgarrif had a tear in his eye as we drove off...

Chapter 15 War!

We got back to Airport Camp and topped up our tans, the humidity of the jungle seemed to wash it off. But I overdid the 'walking around topless' bit and burnt my back, and I didn't realise how bad it was until I had a game of volley ball with the Signals Platoon. When I got back to my room, I put a T shirt on and one of the Signals came in and invited me to make up the numbers in the volley ball game. Why not, it couldn't hurt could it? But it did. The game was OK until one of the players, another Russell, climbed up my back to reach a high ball. I should imagine they heard my blood curdling screams of pain in Mexico City! It was so bad that the skin on my back was no longer on my back; it was attached to my T shirt. The irony is that we call the Signals scaly backs! There was no way I could possibly avoid medical attention and this kind of thing was known as a self-inflicted wound, which was a chargeable offence. Regardless of the consequences, I had to visit the medical centre. The medic who treated my injuries was most sympathetic and understanding. Unfortunately the Medical Officer, who had popped in, wasn't. "You should be charged for this!" he yelled. Personally I couldn't have given a shit because I was in agony. To be fair to the MO, he didn't have me charged and the treatment was done on the quiet. It just meant I had to carry on like everything was normal and all OK. A painful business but at least I wasn't collecting RPs and busted to private.

Once the healing process was well and truly in its stride, I went off into the town. At some point I left my mates and decided to have a chicken and chips supper before catching a taxi back to camp. There was a kind of chippy near the swing bridge so I went there, even though the chicken looked suspiciously like cat. While I was tucking into my supper and looking for a taxi, I was approached by a young lady. She sidled up to me and asked if I would sleep with her. She certainly didn't beat about the bush! To be honest I think she was more interested in a bed for the night rather than my company. We set off in search for a hotel and found one that pinches your towels. For B$15 we got a room with a wall to wall bed and we could just manage to open the door. When I woke up the next morning something wasn't right. It was daylight! We never saw daylight in the camp until after our early morning run! I leapt out of bed, got dressed, may have said goodbye, then grabbed a taxi. I got the driver to drop me off out of sight of the guardroom because I had some serious bluffing to do. I would approach the window and ask if I booked in last night, that way they might think I'd been in camp all night and forgotten to book in. I would say to the guard commander "Did I book in last night?" and he, hopefully, would reply "No you didn't." Then I would say "Tut, tut, how thoughtless of me." Then everything would be fine. So I marched up to the window. "Did I book in last night?" I asked (the plan was working fine). "L/Cpl Russell! Get in a cell!" came the reply (plan unravelling fast now). Later that morning I was in the OCs office collecting a B$15 fine. Thirty dollars for a leg over that I couldn't even remember, it's only twenty in the Big C!

But that was the least of my problems because, as happens in the Army, we found ourselves on the brink of war. When we landed in Belize for our six months tour we didn't account for Guatemala picking a fight. War? It was certainly looking that way. Guatemala was massing its troops on the border and threatened to cross into our playground. "It's just the Guatemalans engaging in a bit of sabre rattling," said our officers.

"War? No it's just sabre rattling. By the way Smith, pack my brown trousers."

Maybe it was and maybe it wasn't, but the Peanut Platoon was split up and sent to the rifle companies at the front. Our small band of Peanut warriors was sent to San Ignacio on the border where we could see the Guatemalans across the river from us. If they were any closer we could have shared rations. On our first day we were taken round the area by the company's OC and he showed us where he wanted the defence positions. Things like trenches, minefields and concertina fencing. While we followed the OC, I couldn't help but notice the patch on his arse pocket - 'don't follow me I'm lost', it said. "Right Sir," I said, "We'll make a start now..." "No, no, no, no, no, no," he said, "Do that and we might stir up the enemy!" Stir them up? If we waited for them to attack we'd be signing our stores over to their Peanut Platoon. But that's the way it was to be.

There were still other preparations to be made, like taking the first pressure off the fuses of our MK7 land mines because they only had light armour. To do this you placed the fuse into a piece of equipment called a 'nutcracker'. Having put the fuse in, you pulled the lever down and the first pressure was off. You only pulled it once, pull it twice and the thing will explode and the user would find it difficult to pull anything after that. This delicate operation was left to Rags Ryder; while we passed the fuses he regaled us with his war stories. At one point the war stories paused and so did Rag's pulling arm. He peered closely at the fuse. "Did I take the first pressure off that one or not?" he asked, and before anyone could voice an opinion he pulled the handle again. Bodies dived in all directions taking cover behind concrete pillars, rocks and Chesty Morgan. Anything. "No, I hadn't!" called Rags who sounded like he was miles away.

The camp was only designed to hold one rifle company so it became a little crowded when us lot and other departments descended on them. This resulted in most of us sleeping in the canteen which doubled up as the camp cinema. That wouldn't have been a bad thing but the supply line was stretched to the limit and films were low on their list of priorities. As a consequence we had to suffer the same film every night. I never want to see 'The Apple Dumpling Gang' ever again! As soon as we got fed up of watching that, we turned to other forms of entertainment, like catching fire flies in match boxes.

During the day we would walk around our area of operations and cast an eye over whatever the enemy were doing. They weren't doing much. Joe Frazier and Chesty Morgan were also evaluating the situation. "If they do cross the border," he said to Chesty, "I'm off into the jungle!" "I'll be with you," replied Chesty, "we could easily survive in there." I looked at the two of them and told them they would never make it. "I don't see why not," said Joe, as he judged the distance between us and the jungle line. "Because I'd have to shoot you in the back for cowardice," I informed him while I stroked my SLR. "You wouldn't do that," they both said. "I'd have to," I told them, "I'm the NCO and that's one of my many responsibilities!" Every time I passed them after that they would view me with suspicion, suddenly they weren't too sure about me. Something that they did find more reassuring was the Harrier jump jets doing barrel rolls up and down the border. These were awesome flying machines, especially when they hovered vertically out of the jungle. Guatemala must have thought we had Thunderbirds on our team!

After a few weeks, the Guatemalans picked up their tanks and went home for tea which meant the war was postponed until another day. This enabled us to return to Airport Camp and resume our normal routine like drinking and fishing. We could also do soldierly things like shooting on the ranges which is where Bill introduced us to 'Ginge'. Ginge was a small man with wild red hair and bushy sideburns and looked a bit like a leprechaun. When we went firing on the range with him he showed us all manner of things, things that would be against the grain with most weapon instructors, and we fired Armalites, Bills pistols and the fall-apart shotgun. We were introduced to SAS style weapon handling and managed to have great fun without shooting ourselves. When I would see Ginge on the camp I'd greet him as Ginge and he called me John. Weeks later I found out he was a Sergeant Major with the SAS! He was a nice bloke but I wouldn't want to get on his wrong side.

The REME had their own drinking club on the camp and they called themselves 'The Water Rats'. It was only because of that drinking club that the REME knew of Vince's existence! It was a warm night when Vince and I returned to camp after a night on the beer and we came across a body on the playing field. It was a dead water rat. Not one of the REME, but a real water rat and it was the size of a medium dog!

After much prodding and poking we decided it really was dead then came up with a drunken idea. We would drag it over to the REME flagpole and hoist it aloft. After all, they were water rats weren't they? Even though it weighed like a sack of spuds we managed to get it to the flagpole and tied the rope to its tail. With a great deal of effort we got it to the top of the pole and tied the rope off. Then we both went to our beds and wished we could be there when one of the REME untied the rope and had a fat rat descending. I saw Vince the following day and he suggested that we kept a low profile and shouldn't really mention our little jape. Apparently the REME were not amused with our antics and if they found out who was responsible for this outrage they would hang them from the flagpole. I think Vince was right, we'd maintain a very low profile...

One afternoon, I was returning to my hut and noticed smoke billowing out of the door and people running about with fire buckets. Someone had left a cigarette burning in an ashtray on his bed and the bedding caught alight. One of our room-mates was most upset, he kept his tarantula in a jar next to his bed and it got knocked over in the melee. He couldn't find his spider anywhere, which stopped me running in there with a bucket. I made a point of not stepping into the room until the fugitive spider was found or declared dead from smoke inhalation. I don't know why they couldn't find it because it was a big, fat furry thing with ginger eyebrows. Not many soldiers look like that... except Rags Ryder maybe. All tarantulas looked like him. The thick black smoke of the burning mattress had got everywhere, it was so bad that we had to clean everywhere and the lockers needed a new coat of paint. Bill told us we would have to paint the lockers ourselves. "What colour?" I asked him. "Any colour you like," said Bill, "as long as its battleship grey." I obviously missed the last bit and painted mine pillar box red and apple green. It certainly stood out in a crowd. It was weeks before it became battleship grey and that was only because Bill threatened to lock me up and throw away the key. That's what I liked about Bill, he'd give you incentive.

There were some Saturday mornings when, after a night on the beer, you just wanted to lie in and die. But Bill didn't see it that way and came crashing in, pulling bedclothes off as he went along, telling us that we were to do some soldiering. Bill, soldiering? On a Saturday morning??

But, being Bill, our soldiering would take the form of a boat trip down the Belize River in one of our assault boats with a big outboard motor. Personally I would have been happier dying in my bed. Just to make it more interesting the Royal Engineers took one of their boats out too. Off we went, heading westward along the river, deep into the jungle. It was a nice trip really where iguanas could be seen lounging on branches and a world of marine life gliding beneath the boat. Bill was admiring the fish when his spectacles decided to part company with his head and fell into the depths. "John!" he shrieked, "Jump in and get me glasses!!" Having a laugh wasn't he? I wasn't going in there and nobody else seemed too keen either, so Bill and his glasses were never to be reunited. At the end of our trip, the engineers decided we would race back to Airport Camp and, because they felt superior, they would give us a head start. Away we went with our outboard motor churning up the water and the breeze in our hair. At the first bend we looked back and saw the engineers waving us off and we managed to get back to the landing stage without clapping eyes on them again. In fact we never saw them again until just before closing time in the NAAFI and they weren't very happy. Apparently they weren't waving us off at the first bend; they were beckoning us back because their outboard packed up. Subsequently they paddled all the way back whereas we could easily have towed them. Worse than that, they missed out on their drinking in the bar.

It would be wrong of me to write about Belize and not mention Alma. Alma was one of those 'employees' in the Big C, a nice lady who must have liked me because I got discount! Vince constantly badgered me about being infatuated with her. I told him it was purely a business arrangement. In the end, to prove him wrong, I snubbed Alma and went with a girl with a face like a slate layer's nail bag. That may have proved a point but Alma never spoke to me again and I lost my discount. Alma, should you ever read this, blame Vince, it was his fault!

July 1977

I'd been married to Pam for almost a year and our first born son would be arriving any time now. We didn't want to miss wetting the baby's head so, to be on the safe side, we went on the beer every night. We did that for a fortnight: me, Vince and Bill. But it all proved too much, even for me, and the drink took its toll. I was whacked and it must have bordered on alcohol poisoning. "Are you coming out tonight John?" Bill and Vince asked. At first I refused but they played the guilt card. "What about wetting the baby's head?" That was a fair argument so I reluctantly agreed, but only on the condition that I drank milk. I'd had enough beer. They both scoffed at this thought of Russell drinking milk but went along with the idea, believing that I would weaken at some point during the night. But I didn't and I drank milk, goat's milk at that, all night long. It was 21st July 1977. How do I remember that? Because that was when my son arrived, he was born the day I was drinking goat's milk! Next morning we had a run. We ran a mile or so down the road, ran back and I ran straight to the shit house. Never ever spend a night on goat's milk. Belikin beer tasted like nectar after that. But now our tour of Belize was coming to an end; six months of Caribbean sunshine and beer.

Before I leave this chapter, I have to mention the unsung hero of our tour, Swampy. Swampy was a 3 ton Bedford truck with a jib. No job was too tough. One day we had a vehicle stuck fast when it came off the track so the MT sent out a vehicle to recover it. That too became stuck. Another vehicle went and that too became a casualty. Then they sent out Swampy which recovered all of them. The lorry was a legend and I'd like to think it went on serving the Army for many more years. I'm sure that any soldier who met it would remember it fondly.

But now I had to go back to Catterick and meet my son, Stuart, for the first time. I loved Belize and one day I would really like to go back there.

Chapter 16 Liverpool and Green Goddesses

The Yorkshire weather greeted us like an old friend, except old friends don't normally lash the skin off your face. Vince Pickup was coming to the end of his service although the REME thought he'd left at the beginning of the Belize tour. I would miss him. My son Stuart was two weeks old when I first met him and now the Battalion were sending me on yet another course. I'd be away for a few weeks and while I was gone the firemen went on strike. It didn't affect me but when I came back the camp was virtually deserted, everyone had gone to Liverpool to cover for the striking firemen on Op Burberry. Well, I seemed to have got out of that one. On my first day back I waltzed into camp and bumped into the OC. "Pack your kit, we're off to Liverpool" he said. Aw shit. Again I said goodbye to Pam and Stuart then headed off with the OC. On our way to Liverpool he explained what my role was, I would travel around the various locations and draw cartoons for Public Relations. Well that beats wrestling with a hose. Most people would see this as a cushy number and take advantage of it. Me? Well I'm like most people really. It was a cushy number and I did have a free rein but, going around the locations, I did see things that restored my faith in human kindness. Like the day at the old drill hall. I was in the company offices and a civilian, a perfect stranger, walked in with two young boys in tow. He wanted to speak to the officer in charge. "I only live over the road," he said, "and if any of your men want to take a shower or watch TV on their night off they're more than welcome to come over." What a nice gesture and what a wonderful man. The people of Liverpool were certainly a hospitable crowd. I'll never forget that.

Because I had to draw these men and machines at work it meant I had to tag along with them when they went 'on a shout'. Normally they would attend skip fires started by youngsters so they could watch the soldiers play with their hoses. (Don't get me wrong, the Army and their green goddesses attended more serious incidents than that!) I went on a call where some small fire had risen up and I stood at the back of the appliance while the lads went about their business of fighting the minor blaze. And that's where I was, at the back of our fire engine wearing a yellow jacket over my civvies, when a lady and her husband came out of a house with a tray of sherry glasses. "Just a little something to warm you up love," she said. "Thank you and cheers Ma'am," I said as I took a glass. The gesture alone was warming, the sherry was a bonus. So there I stood, on a street in Liverpool, sipping a glass of sherry. That's something else you don't see on those recruiting posters! If that lady ever reads this book I can only say that I can't drink a glass of sherry without remembering that night!

The RSM at the time was Regimental Sergeant Major Bill Marshall who was cruelly nick-named 'Clarence' on account he was cross eyed. (You would have to remember the TV series 'Daktari' to pick that one up.) We found out his son was with us and driving Green Goddesses. He was renowned for his driving skills, or rather the lack of, especially with his reversing. We always had the police at the locations so they could escort the appliances to the fires. Every time they parked up before the RSMs son, he would drive in and was like a pin ball machine. He'd bounce off a patrol car and bump one of their motorbikes. Every time he returned to the yard you could guarantee he'd hit one of them. He was quite a legend. In the end, the police stayed clear of the yard until he'd parked up. I saw the RSM one day and asked him how is son was. "Son?!" he said, "I don't have a son!" Whoops. Maybe I caught him on a bad day or maybe the police had given him the repair bill! We often got invited to the police social club; I never saw the RSM or junior there though.

One of the locations I went out to was an old airfield at Birkenhead where I was temporarily reunited with the old Pioneer Platoon. I spotted their green goddess straight away, it was the one with Kermit the Frog hanging in the windscreen. Yes, we were muppet fans. Some would say, rather cruelly, that we were muppets. I could tell that the lads missed me by their greeting. "Jammy bastard!" they would say, obviously jealous of my newfound, but temporary, appointment. I spent most of my time at Birkenhead drawing cartoons of the police. It's nice to take the piss and be appreciated for it! Incidentally, my mother-in-law came from Birkenhead. No wonder I got on with her...

Now and again we would get time off and were able to go into City where we would come across the pickets of firemen. They were OK blokes and they never held it against us that we were doing their job. They would cheer any green goddess that passed by and we wished them luck with their pay claim. Out of interest, it was noted that the Army was working an 84 hour week during Op Burberry but were only earning two-thirds of what the brigade were earning before they went on strike. Perhaps the Queen's shilling should be the Queen's fiver. Depending on inflation of course.

An agreement was finally reached and the firemen went back to work which saw us depart from Liverpool and return to soldiering. Except me, I was a Peanut. My son was now twice as big than when I last saw him. At this rate he'll be bigger than me. Bill, being a big softy, turned up at our house and presented Stuart with the well-travelled Kermit from his fire engine. Kermit remained with our family for many years and has only recently fallen apart with old age. You'll be pleased to know he was buried in the dustbin with full military honours.

The RSM, Bill 'Clarence' Marshal, was still with us and I heard a wonderful story about him. (This was recently confirmed as true by John Edwards via Facebook.) The RSM went into his office one morning and got straight down to his paperwork when there was a knock on his door. It was one of the guard with his morning cup of tea. "Come in!" he bellowed. The soldier, with cup and saucer in hand, walked up to his desk. While still engrossed with his paperwork the RSM shouted "Knee!" By this he meant 'bend the knee' as you would when coming to attention. Obviously he hadn't seen the cup of tea. The soldier thought he said 'kneel' and went down on bended knee. The RSM, not normally flustered, saw him and leapt from his seat. "Stand up man!" he ordered, "I'm not God yet!!" Now they are the kind of stories that made me laugh. Something that didn't make me laugh was a boil I developed on the back of my neck. I didn't mean to, it just happened. I found it was getting quite painful and Pam took a dislike to the sensitive lump so I paid a visit to the Medical Centre. Sergeant John Costain invited me into the treatment room and took a look at the offending object. "Mmm," he said, "that's a big one!" Then he took a scalpel out of its wrapper and moved in on the target. "Whoa!" I said, "Don't I get a local anaesthetic first?" John Shrugged. "Only if you really want one," he said indifferently. "I do, I really do!" I told him. After all this is the modern Army, we're not Barbarians. With a sigh he went to his medical cabinet and came back with a syringe. Have you, the reader, ever had an injection in the neck? Let me tell you it bloody hurts! God, it was like having a red hot poker thrust in there. John set about the carbuncle with his scalpel. That only took a few seconds and then he grabbed me round the neck and squeezed for all he was worth. I thought he was going to kill me for making him use a valuable hypodermic. Then 'pop'. "Wow!" said John, "Look at that go!" If it was all the same to him I won't bother. After that one sided wrestling match I left there with a stiff neck and a headache. Next time I get a boil I'll keep it to myself.

"The boil? Oh that went ten minutes ago!"

I continued working in the Peanut Platoon and, after several years at Catterick, it was time to get posted again. This pleased Pam because, although she liked the Army life, she wasn't too struck with the Garrison here. She was looking forward to our new posting so we all packed our bags and headed to south to Dover.

Chapter 17 White Cliffs and Canada Geese

January 1978

Pam was hoping for a more exotic posting but for now we'd have to make do with Dover. We were initially housed in Folkestone at the top of a hill called Oxenden Way, with us at the top and a pub at the bottom. The pub was 'The Golden Arrow' and it was a pleasure to walk down there. But, in the winter, it was hell getting back up with a pushchair and snow underfoot. It was a bit like uphill skiing. There were a few of us in Folkestone, they were still building the quarters in Dover, and every morning a three ton truck would pick us up and transport us to Connaught Barracks. Connaught was situated just behind Dover Castle and was a lot smaller in comparison to Catterick Garrison (sadly the barracks no longer exists). We Peanuts had an office opposite the main gate next to the guardroom with the armoury and a small yard behind us. At the back of the camp was Fort Burgoyne, an old fortress which housed our stores and allowed us to play with booby traps in privacy. Over the road were the Officers Mess and a 30 metre range. I often thought having a range running alongside a public road was a bit dodgy but we had no civilian casualties while we were there! All in all, Dover turned out to be a nice posting and Pam was to enjoy it tremendously.

Sergeant Bill Dixon decided that our stocks of explosive had mounted up so we needed to whittle it down a bit. That warranted a day out on the demolition range at Yantlet. We piled boxes of explosive in a truck and plenty of detonators in the escorting Land Rover, then left for the range. We also had an officer with us who came along for the ride. When we arrived at the range we were greeted by a very irritable range warden. "Now listen," he said to Bill, "you go down to the range and play with your explosives but there's a new gate on the bridge and I want it in one piece when you leave! The bloody commandos keep blowin' the bugger off!" Bill assured him that the gate was safe with us; we were far too professional for that kind of nonsense. We pulled up in our truck and looked around the area. A small stream meandered through the deserted grounds with a footbridge crossing it and there was indeed a nice new gate on there. So we'll leave that alone then. We unpacked our big bangs and Bill assigned me to an old telegraph pole sticking out of the ground. "Scissor charge on there," he said and left me with a few pounds of PE4. A scissor charge is when you place the explosive on each side of the pole, slightly offset. When it explodes it cuts through the pole much like a pair of scissors would. Simple ain't it? As I set about my mission, Bob Keen came along with a barrow full of explosives and told me I had to use some more because Bill was worried about having too much left over. At the end of it I had a telegraph pole with two huge bulges of explosive dripping off it. Our guest Officer wandered over my way and inspected my work of art. "What's the idea behind this then?" he asked. I explained to him the theory behind my creative masterpiece. "And this will do the job?" he queried. I looked at the mass of explosive gripping the pole. "Do it Sir?" I said, "I think it might just do it." After we finished setting all of our charges we retired to the regulation 1000 metre firing point and set the whole lot off. The sky was suddenly full of debris and plumes of grey smoke and we reckon the bang probably rattled the windows in Downing Street. We returned to the scene of devastation and my telegraph pole was now a crater and lots of match sticks. Both me and the Officer peered into the huge crater. "Well, that seemed to do the job," he remarked. "Put it this way Sir," I said, "if it was holding up a bridge it ain't now."

"Do it Sir? Yes, I think it might just do it."

Bill was poring over our stocks of explosives; there was still a mountain of them to get rid of. Then we espied an old Mini sat on its roof next to another crater. We all gathered around round the vehicle like a flock of vultures sizing up a carcass. The plan was simple; we would pile all the ordnance into the crater and roll the car onto it. That way we would be rid of our excess bangs and the car would be recycled into the atmosphere. So that's what we did. With the charge set and the vehicle in place we went back 1000 metres and pressed the button. We stood there and witnessed the biggest car bomb in history, a monumental bang. My dad was probably sat in his house reading his Coventry Telegraph and wondering why his window panes were rattling. We returned to the crater and now it was a much bigger crater with no sign of the Mini or anything that resembled a car whatsoever. The whole thing had vaporised. This was job satisfaction and we all congratulated ourselves on a job well done. Then someone spoilt our moment. "Oh shit!" he said, and pointed to the gate on the bridge. Or he would have done if there was a gate. We reckon the engine block had left the scene at mach 3 and flew through the nice new gate. A small bit of splintered wood hung from a bent hinge. Oh shit indeed. Our lorry pulled up at the range warden's hut and Bill turned to me. "Tell the warden we've finished now," he said. "Oh, and tell him…" "You tell him!" I replied. I found it easy to drop myself in the shit, I didn't need Bill's help.

Back at Connaught Barracks we were informed that the Battalion would be performing a 'beating of the retreat' parade and we would be doing the pyrotechnic display. It would be a spectacle that the good people of Dover would remember. The parade would take place in the confines of Fort Burgoyne which had ramps leading up either side. They wanted burning torches to highlight the ramps so our first problem was to get these beacons to ignite on cue at the touch of a button. After fooling around with electric fuses and four million boxes of Swan Vestas we came close to achieving this. The finale would be the band playing Star Wars which would be accompanied by a GPMG and exploding PE4 in the background. We found a safe site to place the explosives to the rear of the fort and, on the night, I would be setting them off. The big day arrived and we went about our business setting everything up. Bob Keen would be in charge of the self-lighting torches, I had the big bangs and someone else was on the GPMG. We also had a band member with us who could read music. If a burst of machine gun fire was required he would say "Fire." If he wanted an explosion he would say "Bang." Everything was set and that evening the public arrived and took their seats while a mob of schoolboys arrived and stood on the top of the fort in their gabardine rain coats. They'll be worth watching when my bangs go off! The band struck up with some suitable military music and marched into the fort to start the proceedings off. As daylight faded, Bob set off his magical self-lighting torches. Except they didn't all ignite. Bob, being ever resourceful, crawled along the row of torches with a box of matches, lighting them as he went. We would like to think that nobody noticed. Then the band began playing Star Wars and my musical debut was fast approaching. "Fire," said the bandsman and the gunner let rip with a short burst. Unfortunately, we Peanuts use the term to detonate so one of my charges blew too. So I started off with a bum note and all the gabardine raincoats flapped on top of the fort. And so it continued, the odd burst of machine gun fire interspersed with the occasional boom until it reached its grand finish. To round the whole thing off we had a Harrier jump jet arrive over the parade square which bowed to the crowd. That was good, except that the parade square was being used as a public car park and a lot of people drove home that night with a pebble dash finish on their motors. But the night was a resounding success, regardless of my bum note.

Nice to see the public turn out!

It was all very well being in the Peanut Platoon but, now and again, we were required to play soldiers so that the top brass could see that we could still fire guns and disguise ourselves as bushes. So we made a visit to a rifle range with our trusty SLRs. While we waited to go onto the main firing range we were taken to one side and shown the jungle trail. This was a small live firing range which consisted of a track going through a wooded area. An individual would walk the trail with the range-safety NCO behind him and behind the NCO, someone who pulled the targets up with a cable. That was always a giveaway because you saw the grass move before the targets came up. So it came to me to patrol down into the woods. Sure enough, you saw a line of undergrowth point the way to the imminent target. I fired a round from standing then took cover to fire a second. But then something took me by surprise, something totally unexpected. As I walked down the track there was a crash of rustling foliage that came from my right. I swung round to see a 'sandbag man' crossing my path on a zip wire with its arms and legs thrashing about! I should have shot it but I was too busy pissing myself laughing. "You're dead!" shouted the NCO. He was close to the truth, I nearly died laughing. The imagination of the Army knows no bounds.

Bill Dixon would soon be departing from our happy band of Peanuts, he had wangled a posting to somewhere in the Middle East. But before then we had another job to do - blowing up Officers at Sandhurst. We would be laying on an artillery simulation for one of their exercises so we loaded up with a shed load of PE4 once again and headed out of camp. On the training area at Sandhurst, we broke our 8oz sticks of explosive into 4oz sticks and placed them in an area that was marked off with white tape. I thought it would be more realistic without the marker tape but it was a safety thing apparently. With the charges laid out we would hide under an old piece of Land Rover canvas, hidden from view but virtually on top of the explosives. So we tape off the area for the safety of the Officers and we sit on top of them. Makes perfect sense. Soon the trainee Officers came marching up the hill and we set off our artillery bombardment, bangs shattering the silence and clumps of earth flying everywhere. Although we were reasonably safe from these exploding special effects there was a problem with the blast wave. I was fine because I wore Amplivox ear defenders, but other people like Jim Prior, only had the general issued ear plugs. It stopped him going deaf but the blast wave pushed them deeper into his lug holes. But after a quick trip to the Medical Centre they were successfully extracted. We spent most of our time in an urban village, a small place built of breeze blocks where soldiers trained in urban warfare, and this was where I learnt a thing or two about cooking with Reg Ryder. Cooking our own individual rations on a hexi burner was a pain in the arse so Rags took it on. He got a thunderflash tin and poured everything in it; Chicken supreme, steak and kidney pudding, rice pudding, processed cheese and just about everything else we had. Then he would take an 8oz stick of plastic explosive and set light to it. My jaw hit the floor as the white, waxy stick burnt furiously. It was a bright reddish/orange flame that crept down its length. "Is that safe?" I asked him. "Ooh, about one in 99 might explode," he replied. "How many times have you done this?" "I've done it hundreds of times," he told me. Well, it didn't explode but you had to be quick cooking in a thunderflash tin otherwise you'd have a hole in the bottom! The result? Surprisingly, Rags' goulash was rather nice! While all this was going on we came across a member of the Royal Engineers who happened to pass through our camp. "Are you OK mate?" we asked. He looked a little concerned and told us he had lost a land grader. For those of you who have never met a land grader it's a huge vehicle that they use to plane the ground when building roads, a humongous vehicle. Apparently he had camouflaged the thing and now he couldn't find it. I can only imagine that he got the highest possible award for his camouflage and concealment skills, followed by a big Court Martial for losing such an expensive piece of kit if he didn't find it! So we had a great day blowing would-be Officers up and Jim got his ear plugs back in his pocket. Everybody was happy.

On our return to Dover, Bill Dixon left us for the United Arab Emirates and Sergeant 'enery Green BEM came as his replacement. It was always a tradition that the Pioneer Sergeant sported a beard, Bill wore his with pride and it had a life of its own. But our 'enery would have none of that; he liked to show off his chin. However he did settle for a rather grand handle-bar moustache. Breaking with tradition? We would have to keep an eye on 'enery.

"The Pioneer Sergeant doesn't HAVE to have a beard! Now let's blow something up."

June 1978

No sooner had Sergeant Green joined us than we were told we would be leaving for Canada on exercise Pond Jump West. Once again I said goodbye to Pam and Stuart, packed my polyester socks into my mess tins and prepared to move. But it was only for four weeks or so. Canada was a wonderful place and I'm sure it still is. It was huge, so big that you could easily mislay the UK in there and never see it again. We were based in Wainwright Camp in Alberta, the sort of place where you would expect cowboys to be having a shootout. The training areas were so vast that we could happily conduct live firing without shooting anybody we shouldn't. I'm sure the locals would be pleased to hear that. But we were the Peanut Platoon and we had our own role to play.

A mile or so from the camp was Mott Lake and we had a couple of assault boats and outboard motors down there. It wasn't an operational thing (although it got people used to being thrown about in boats!) it was more of a leisure activity. Now and again the real soldiers would pop down and we would blast them around the lake. I was walking back from there one day and started to suffer some serious pain in my ankle. I kept walking but the pain got worse and I thought "That's OK, somebody will pass by soon and pick me up out of sympathy." But they were clearly enjoying themselves on the boating lake too much and no vehicles came by. By the time I got back to camp I felt like a cripple and hobbled straight to the Medical Centre. The medic just told me to rest it. "It'll be fine in the morning," he said. But it wasn't fine in the morning, it felt worse. I saw the MO and he diagnosed that my Achilles tendon had gone a burton, and then put me on light duties. A fat lot of good that was for my painful ankle because everyone on light duties had to parade before the RSM every morning. "What's your problem?" he asked me. "Achilles tendon." I told him. He thought that wasn't a big problem and had us all area cleaning. So I spent every morning dragging my ankle through the camp picking up litter and shit. One morning, after picking up crap, I was resting on my bed when the accommodation storeman walked in. "Come and look at this!" he said and invited me into the toilets. (I was safe, he was married!) I followed him in and he pointed to a giant turd in the toilet bowl. "See that?!" he said, as if I could miss it, "That's a sixteen pounder! They were made obsolete in the 60's!" Then he pondered who could have given birth to such a thing. "He shouldn't be too difficult to find," I told him, "Just look for someone walking bandy." Only a squaddie could slag off a turd and derive some pleasure from it. By the end of the week, my ankle was pretty much OK so I joined the platoon before they went into the field.

Basil Pratt was our Padre and no, I didn't just make that up. He was a real down to earth man-of-the-cloth and would often eat in the ORs canteen rather than the Officers Mess. Quite often, he would plonk himself down at a table only for everyone sitting there to get up and move. I don't know why, if he sat at our table we welcomed him. I asked him why he didn't eat in the Officers Mess with his fellow Officers. "What?" he replied, "Why would I want to eat with that lot for? I prefer eating with the men!" It's a shame that they didn't feel the same. On the morning of the big exercise, Basil held a church service on the parade ground. He stood in front of the Battalion and began his sermon which started off like any other. Then he seemed to stray off the footpath of the righteousness and went into a very strange diatribe. I don't remember the exact words he used but you wouldn't find them in the Bible. These were naughty words. Very naughty words. At the end of his address he got a rousing cheer, a first for a Padre I should think. Good old Basil. It's funny but we didn't see him after that.

Out in the field, our first task was to dig a hole for a thunderbox in the middle of nowhere. The whole Battalion would be passing by at various times and it would be nice if they could have a comfortable shit. There was no time limit on this so we just kept digging towards the centre of the earth. We dug so far down that the last man had to raise his shovel with his outstretched arm in order for us to pull him out. I said we should leave him in there but someone cited the Geneva Convention, something to do with a biological warfare clause. The big hole was crowned with a beautifully crafted shed and stood like a monument on the prairie. We asked if it could stay there for all mankind to admire, with a brass plaque to honour our unstinting devotion, and perhaps become a listed building of historical importance. But we were told it would fall foul of hygiene regulations.

After that we had to head out to one of the rifle company positions and lay charges for a simulated artillery attack. But these weren't lumps of PE4, these were big cardboard containers packed with gunpowder and we were assured that they would make an acceptable bang. For some odd reason Sergeant 'enery Green decided we would approach the position tactically, on foot and in the dark. This was a novelty indeed so I went as tail end Charlie and tagged onto the end of the line, making sure my mates didn't get shot up the arse. Every now and again the man in front of me would whisper "get down", so I would get down facing to the rear. Then he would say "We're moving" so I'd get up and move behind them. This was OK until about 02:00 hrs when my man in front told me to get down. I got down and stayed down. I seemed to be down for a long while and wondered what was going on. After half an hour I heard hurried footsteps coming from the direction of the patrol. "John! John!" said a disembodied voice in the darkness. "Over here!" I said,

"What's happening?" My patrol buddy knelt beside me. "We moved thirty minutes ago!" he said, "We thought we'd lost you!" Well that's a fine thing, here I am making sure they don't get shot in the arse and they bugger off and leave me! There's gratitude for you.

We reached the company position and got our heads down for a few hours. When daylight came we started to dig D10 into the ground and concealing it (D10 is a single strand wire that the Signals use for field phones and such like). If anybody became too nosey and asked what we were doing, I'd tell them we were routing cables for the Signals. That seemed to satisfy their curiosity, but they didn't see the cardboard bucket of gunpowder on the end of it. By the end of our digging we had many wires and many cardboard buckets in place. All we had to do now was sleep until just before daybreak... We all woke up and daylight was about to make an appearance so we shuffled off to our firing points. With contacts and wires at the ready, we waited for the word and it wasn't long before it came. One after the other the charges exploded filling the air with clumps of earth and acrid smoke, numerous tent pegs whistling through the air. One hell of an early morning call! Bodies piled out of their tents and ran amok, blasting away at an unseen enemy. I've never witnessed panic like that since. I got a bollocking for that. 'Enery told me I should have warned them about it. Would a real enemy pop over and tell them of their plans? I think not.

Our next task was a bigger one; we had to build a bridge across a river so that the troops and their vehicles could cross. We went off and looked at the location and we reckoned the river was all of thirty feet from one bank to the other. That would be some bridge. The best of it was that we didn't have anything to build it with! Our 'enery said we could build it and struck a deal with the CO. "When we build it," he told the CO, "and when we get the troops and their vehicles over we want to be called Combat Engineers, not Assault Pioneers." Amazingly the CO agreed, probably because he didn't think we could do it. So we got to work. We had four days to complete the task and our first problem was the river bank on the opposite side of the river, it was too steep and we needed to level it out. PE4 would have been useful but we didn't have any with us. Then Dave Wildman reminded everyone that we still had some of those artillery pyrotechnics we'd used on the rifle companies. Why not, they were gunpowder weren't they? We dug a few holes in the bank and pushed home some of the charges. Dave was the last one to come wading across the river but we couldn't wait for him so we set them off. There was an almighty bang and Dave ran across the surface of the water with a big brown shower of shit chasing him. When he got back to us he was laughing his head off. I reckon if we blew his head off he would still have found it funny.

Dave 'Borneo' Wildman attempts the water speed record on foot

After a few more blasts and some digging we had ourselves a fairly reasonable approach. As night fell we stayed out on the area with our sleeping bags and a supply of Labatt beer for company. As we lay there we watched the Northern Lights (Aurora Borealis). It was a wonderful sight, like net curtains swaying in the night sky. Truly beautiful. Next morning we started to build the supporting piers using corrugated sheets, angle iron pickets and rocks. While we did that, Dave went berserk with a chain saw and dragged some trees over. Over the next few days we worked hard and the bridge began to take shape. On the last day we had our bridge but we needed some planks to finish it off. Well we did get some planks and we lashed them down. If you are wondering where we got planks from in the middle of nowhere then let me just say that there was a perfectly serviceable bridge 500 yards upstream. The less said about that the better. Just after dark the spearhead of the Battalion arrived, all of whom marched over our bridge. Then the rest of the Battalion came along with the vehicles. We got all of the men over and one Land Rover. We told the CO that we could easily get the other vehicles over too but he felt he'd pushed his luck far enough for one night! However, he did bestow upon us the title of Combat Engineers. (I know my old mate Blue Cooper will hate that story. Blue would one day be the Pioneer Sergeant and, as far as he's concerned, the Peanuts would forever be Assault Pioneers! Sorry about that Blue but at least you know where the cookhouse is.)

Our short visit to Canada was now over and we found our 'enery to be a decent bloke who didn't mind mucking in with the rest of us. If only he could shake off that soldiering business...

September 1978

After a few weeks leave, giving me time with Pam and Stuart, we were to be moving off on another exercise. This was Exercise Bold Guard and we would be travelling to Schleswig-Holstein in Germany. It was a huge multinational exercise and our accommodation would be tents, thousands of them, near Flensburg. I was told that this was the biggest movement of troops since WWII. I always found it difficult to remember which my tent was amongst the thousands of identical tents. On the rare occasions we were allowed down to the village it was a nightmare finding my own sleeping bag. And then I hoped there was nobody else in it! We had some members of the TA with us and I got on well with them, probably because of our shared interest in the local beer. I recall one was a bank manager, another was a mechanic and the third was a road sweeper. Regardless of their backgrounds they were like old mates. They probably wouldn't give each other the time of day back home, but here they were comrades in arms. Most of our time on exercise was spent laying minefields and other defensive obstacles and, unlike Canada which was warm and welcoming, this was cold rain and oppressive. One night, after laying cardboard bar mines, we had the pleasure of sleeping out under the stars. Except we couldn't see the stars for rain clouds and the rain came down like stair rods. In the morning I woke up, unzipped my green maggot and floated out with the gallons of water I had slept with. No way to start the day. Having spent the day travelling through wet forests and muddy tracks we pulled up in a village square, only a small village but it had a pub. First we got some beer in for those stuck with the truck then half would pop over for a few comfortable pints. Half way through the night we would swap, or that was the plan. Dave Wildman was my opposite number and when he came back I could have a few pints in there. But Dave got too comfortable and I don't think PE4 would have shifted him off his bar stool. He only came back because it was closing time and they threw him out. Shame on him, it should have been me they were throwing out! After a few weeks of roughing it we all went back to Dover.

The new quarters at Burgoyne heights were now finished so Pam and I packed up our things along with Stuart and moved again, this time we were at 184 Kohima Place. Now we lived a stone's throw from the camp I could have a bit of a lie in every morning

Northern Ireland was always lurking in the background so a lot of our training was aimed in that direction. Lydd and Hythe ranges were just down the road and we also had the Close Quarter Battle range there. The CQB range was imaginatively built like a horse shoe shaped street and decorated to look like Northern Ireland with things like 'Paddy McGintys pub' and 'Seamus the butcher'. The street was furnished with all manner of things: a car that the starter motor could be operated from the control room and a mannequin that went across the butcher's shop window. There was another mannequin in the toilets who turned around, sometimes with a gun in his hand, other times holding a carrot. (Regardless what he carried, the .22 holes in his head bore testament to the fact that he was very unpopular!) Our job was to set up the bangs, bullet splats and other effects. We used, amongst other things, No6 detonators and our old friends the powder puff gunpowder bags. The puff bags would be wired up in a strategically placed dustbin but, because it had been used so many times, the battered lid didn't sit on the bin, it sat in it. This often became a very life-threatening object flying aimlessly around the range. One night we were waiting for the next section to come through and, while I sat in the small kitchen, I noticed a rat. He was using his furry little chin to roll away a discarded tomato.

"Cheeky little sod," I thought then set about making a booby trap using a No6 detonator and cunningly disguising it as a tomato. Satisfied that it was all wired up I went back to my book, Rambo, First Blood. After about 10 minutes there was a bang which got everyone running to the kitchen, maybe they thought I'd shot myself. We looked at the rat and it just lay there motionless. But he would, his head had gone AWOL. Then the troops turned up for the range.

Because this was the last section to pass through for the night we'd put the remainder of the puff bags in the dustbin to get rid of them, about five or six of them. What harm could it do? As the patrol went through they had everything thrown at them with bullet splats going off all over the place. Then one unfortunate soul, Tyrone Power, took cover behind our dustbin. Just as he moved off, we detonated the charge and he disappeared in a cloud of smoke with the dustbin lid flying off down the street.

Tyrone Power takes cover behind 'our' dustbin!

When the smoke cleared we could see Tyrone and he was staggering in a most peculiar fashion and we thought we'd maimed him! But no, at the de-brief he explained that he was wearing nylon underpants and when the blast went off the heat shrunk them! Who could have imagined that? And what a thing to call the end of exercise chat, a debrief!

Back in Connaught Barracks things went on in their usual routine sort of way. This, of course, involved drawing cartoons. This wasn't an official duty it was something I did now and again to keep me out of trouble. Sometimes it got me into trouble, like when I drew a cartoon of one of the NCOs. I don't remember his name but the RQMS was WOII 'Mickey' Wishhussen and everywhere the RQMS went so too did the NCO. So I drew a cartoon showing the NCO with his head down the back of the RQMS's trousers with the caption 'Sorry Sir, I couldn't hear you, you sounded muffled'. I think it must have ended up pinned on the notice board because it came to the attention of the NCO concerned and he took it to the RQMS complaining about "Russell and his poisonous little pen!" After being summoned, I stood in front of the RQMS. He sat behind his desk with the incriminating doodle in his hand. He looked at the cartoon then looked at me. "You really should be careful with your drawings," he said, "Some people can get quite upset." He carried on and I don't know whether it was a bollocking or not because he was smirking. In the end he dismissed me from his office, but not before asking me if he could keep the cartoon! Of course he could.

Something else warranted a cartoon, something which may have involved the RQMS or it could have been an officer. Regardless of whom it was, the person concerned drove into the camp and the barrier was raised by the sentry. I'm told the sentry may have been Jimmy Johncock. The barrier was a manually operated one where you pushed down the weighted end and held it there. The driver of the car pulled up alongside Jimmy and told him to stand to attention which was befitting of the driver's rank. Well poor Jimmy stooped there, his rifle in one hand and his other holding the barrier. But he was a good soldier so he stood to attention… and watched the barrier crash onto the car. Sometimes it feels good to obey orders.

Chapter 18 From Peanuts to Squirrels

October 1978

Being in the Combat Engineers, sorry Blue, I meant the Assault Pioneers, was an interesting experience and I'd had fun. But the grass was beginning to grow under my feet and I had a mate, Sergeant Tony Gittins, who was in the Intelligence Section. He told me there was a vacancy in the section for a draughtsman. I didn't know anything about technical drawing but I could draw a mean cartoon so Tony arranged an interview for me with the Intelligence Officer (IO) who was Captain Mills. He was an approachable Officer and we had a very nice chat where he agreed to have me transferred. Before I left his office he told me one more thing. "Remember L/Cpl Russell," he said, "intelligence in the Army is only an appointment, not a state of mind." Oh good, I can live with that. Within a few short weeks I was transferred.

On my first day Tony introduced me to my new workmates, Pete Gerrard, Ivan Jellis and Dougie Douglas. Pete was a likeable man and was probably more worthy of the intelligence label than any of us. Ivan was our photographer and no, he wasn't Russian, he hailed from The Isle Of Wight. Dougie was, well he was Dougie. Collectively we were known as The Secret Squirrels. I was largely responsible for drawing up diagrams to show how enemy forces were organised, or ORBATS. Maps and training pamphlets also came under our control. I lost count of how many amendments we made to training pamphlets, we had a lorry load every week!

But things were changing, not only did we have Northern Ireland to contend with but there were also other aspects of modern warfare - just in case a real enemy started a real war. It was decided that I would attend a Nuclear, Biological and Chemical warfare course (NBC). More than that it was an instructor's course, which meant attending Porton Down and returning to train the Battalion. What an awesome responsibility.

January 1979

Yet again I left Pam and my son, who was 18 months old now, and went off to Porton Down. Here I would train to teach soldiers the art of NBC defence. I would also learn how to plot and predict atomic fallout and a lot about weather conditions which affected all sorts of things. I was very apprehensive about the course but I needn't have worried because I and everyone else involved were in the same boat. Also on the course was Sergeant Major Bird who, I believed, came from 2 Queen's. He was a nice happy bloke, happier when he was leading me astray. One of the first things they tell you is if you expect your students to wear a respirator then, as the instructor, so should you. I took that on board but a Sergeant from The Irish Rangers clearly didn't. This Sergeant stood at the rear of an old APC shell and was giving a lesson in suit changing drills and while his pupils were wearing respirators, he wasn't. That was a pity really because Sergeant Major Bird had an aerosol of CS gas in his possession. Now if you think for one minute that a Sergeant Major from the Queen's Regiment would use this spray in such a situation you would be very wrong. No, he passed it to me instead. He nodded at the aerosol and nodded toward the respirator-less Sergeant. Not wanting to disappoint my fellow Queensman I slipped off to one side of the vehicle and peered through the gap of the rear door hinges. It only took one squirt. The Irish Sergeant was going into great detail about changing trousers when he broke into a convulsive coughing fit with tears and snot flying in all directions.

Never trust a Sergeant Major when learning NBC

It's not easy to laugh in a respirator, the rubber seal slaps on your skin. And that's all you could hear, rubber slapping on skin. The Sergeant, having aired himself, returned to us. "Who the fuck did dat!?" he raged. All I heard was the muffled 'He did' from the Sergeant Major's respirator as he pointed in my direction. The Sergeant strode over to me and pulled himself up to his full 5'4". "Do dat again an' you'll be wearing dem fuckin' balls fer earrings!!" he bellowed. A menacing silence lingered then there was the slapping of rubber on face from the Sergeant Major's direction...

"Good grief! Was that a sneeze?!"

We spent a lot of our time in the lecture theatre split into syndicates. A recording would play giving a warning of bombardment or air attack and we would have to don our respirators and begin the business of plotting and predicting, poring over our maps and being fed more information. Prior to these attacks the tea lady would stroll in with her trolley and serve up tea and coffee. I was there, in my respirator, problem solving with my wind speeds and weather conditions when I suddenly became aware of all these black rubber faces around the room. But my attention was drawn to the bloke reaching for his cup of tea. The cup stopped with a 'clunk' as it hit his rubber mask. Someone tried to work out how he was going to smoke his cigarette that he'd just lit up. The situation looked so absurd that I just laughed; the sort of laughing urge you get at funerals and other events where you know you shouldn't. There was a lot of rubber slapping on face over that.

Our introduction to mustard gas was a memorable moment. The real instructors sat us in a wire compound, well it was a patch of grass with a chain link fence surrounding it, and they dug out a lump of turf. We were told to don our respirators and watched as they opened a container and poured its contents onto the turf. The grass roots curled up and died and an ominous cloud came our way. We all sat there hoping our respirators were working OK. As the gas cloud passed over us and the fence, the instructor assured us that the gas was now inert. If it was OK with him I'd keep my gas mask on a little longer. I felt a little cheated at this stage because on previous courses the students would have a drop of this mustard gas put on their wrist. They would then walk, not run, around the perimeter of the compound with a blister growing ever larger on their skin. Then you would burst the blister and decontaminate the affected area. This left you with a small scar, a badge of honour that said you were an NBC instructor. A bit like a tattoo without the ink. But, due to an ongoing claim by a former soldier, they had stopped this practice by the time I got there. I was robbed of my official scar.

As well as learning to teach NBC we were also expected to work in our NBC suits. For one of these exercises a driver arrived in his Land Rover and parked up. We, as a team, had to change the wheels and rotate them all, a challenging task in full NBC suits and rubber gloves but we did it. The driver, a trusting sort, jumped into his vehicle and drove off. If it was me I would have checked my wheel nuts. Marching back to camp we half expected to see the same vehicle sitting on its axles and his wheels rolling down the road.

The NAAFI was a small bar run by a wonderful lady who didn't understand the concept of 'last orders'. Consequently most of us would stagger out through the door in the early hours. How anybody passed the course I'll never know. Having finished the course someone decided we would have a fancy dress party to say thank you to the manageress and drink lots of her beer. A fancy dress party? When you get your course joining instructions they tell you what is required and I don't remember 'Mickey Mouse costume' being listed on there. I suppose I could have gone as a soldier, or I could go as... One of the WRACs on the course was most obliging as she loaned me her clothes. Did I mention that I didn't make a habit of this sort of thing? Well we had a great night and left the bar at some unearthly hour of the morning with 'Please don't go' by KC and the Sunshine Band ringing in our ears. In the morning we all parted company and went our separate ways, probably never to meet again sadly.

Back in Dover, new friends were made. There was Paul and Diane Nicholson, John and Esther Head and Brian Cunliffe to name a few. Best of all, we were all neighbours and we all enjoyed a drink! Parties were aplenty and it wouldn't be the first time I'd crawled out of someone's house and went straight on duty. Now that's what I call dedication.

Pam and I also made many friends in Dover itself. One couple ran the William of Orange pub so we found ourselves in there a lot. I wish I could remember their names because they're both worth a mention. Every night we were in there and the gaffer would call last orders and start locking the doors. The first time he did this Pam and I drank up. "Not you two," he said, "stay and have another. If the police come knocking tell them you're staff." Neither of us were the sort to argue so we stayed. We also met a chap in there who was the Harbour Master for Dover. After drinking in the pub one night, he asked if we would like to go to his place for a drink or two. We agreed and went walking up the High Street and came across what looked like a deserted bingo hall. "In here," he said and we followed him up the stairs to a door where he produced a key and let himself in. I thought it was odd that he lived in an old bingo hall but I thought it was even stranger when he opened the door and the place was full of people drinking and dancing. It wasn't his house, of course, it was a private drinking club where the harbour workers drank because of the unsociable hours they worked. They should have one of those for soldiers! We had a great night and God only knows what time we left.

Most of my working days were spent teaching the finer points of NBC defence and drawing up charts but, looming up fast, was the Battle Fitness Test. Normally it wouldn't have been much of a problem but, here in Dover, the course took us out to Guston and a most unforgiving hill. That hill hated me. Time and time again I ran out to Guston and time and time again the hill beat me. There were three soldiers who felt the same so they hitched a ride on the way back. Unfortunately the PTI, Mick Jeng, saw them getting out of the car and they got their arses kicked. I thought they would have got medals for showing initiative. Mick Jeng was a PTI Sergeant and, when he wasn't torturing soldiers with fitness training, was a nice bloke. He called me down to the gym one day in the hope of getting me through the BFT. I walked into his little office and he invited me to take a seat. Then he pulled out a sheet of paper and gave it to me. On it was written a poem, an ode to a PTI. "What do you think?" he asked after I read it. I told him it was very nice. Then he asked if I could write it out all nicely so that he could frame it. "I can," I said, "but I've got to get through this BFT first." "Don't worry about that," he said and gave me a fountain pen. I recall thinking "This is the way to pass the BFT" and sat there writing his poem out. When I'd finished I passed it to him. "Wonderful!" he said, "Now about that BFT." If I thought for one minute that I was going to get off light I was wrong. After all this was Mick Jeng and he made a living out of making soldiers suffer. First he ran me ragged around the empty gym then tortured me with the multi-gym. After that he had me on the wall bars making me do things which nearly burst my innards. Not being satisfied with that he stuck my head under a running tap, took a look at me and declared that I looked suitably knackered. "Passed!" he said. I was absolutely worn out; it would have been easier to face that hill.

Being with the Int Cell it meant we had to work alongside the training wing and were expected to run the ranges, whether it was the firing range or the grenade range. Tony Gittins and myself ran the grenade range one day and when the troops arrived we would take them through the safety drills. Well Tony was an entertaining sort of bloke so he decided that this would be best served by a demonstration. Tony played his role of instructor while I played the stupid soldier, a part that came very easily to me. He would explain how to throw the grenade, while I would fumble the drill grenade and drop it in the trench where we were standing. Tony would then leap into action, grab hold of me and throw me and him into the safety bay. Tony seemed to enjoy that immensely. Other times, just for variety, I would throw the pin and drop the grenade in the trench. Tony would do his thing and, more often than not, we would both end up in a pile giggling like schoolgirls.

On another day, I had to run the grenade range with an Officer. He merely explained the safety drills in a boring, monotone fashion. Where was the fun in that? At one point we had a blind, a grenade that didn't explode. At that point everything grinds to a halt because you had to wait something like 20 minutes before destroying it. After the regulation period the Officer approached the dud grenade, placed the charge of PE4 and came back to me at the trench. "Do you have a light?" he asked. "Would you like me to care of it Sir?" I asked. He declined my offer so I passed him my box of England's Glory. I watched as my matches dwindled dangerously low, at this rate I wouldn't be able to light my fags. So I went over to offer my expertise. "It's no good," he said as he stood up, "the fuse must be damp." I took my penknife out, scarfed the fuse, placed the head of a match against the core and struck it with the box. The fuse fizzed happily. The Officer ran back to the safety of the trench. "Hurry man! Hurry!" he shouted. "Never run from a set charge," I mumbled and hoped the bloody thing didn't explode before I got to the trench. With the blind successfully destroyed we continued with the training.

Now again we squirrels were required to spend time out in the field to hone our skills. We did this from our 'mobile office' in the back of a Land Rover which allowed us to have home comforts like a constant flow of decent coffee, a loaf of bread and toilet paper. Prior to one of these exercises Tony thought it would be nice to have a bottle of cheap brandy to be included in those home comforts so he asked Dougie to pop into the town and get one. "What brandy?" asked Dougie. "Any," said Tony, "as long as it's cheap." Dougie reappeared later that afternoon clutching a bottle of Remy Martin. Tony almost fainted. "Cheap? You call that cheap??" yelled Tony, clearly unhappy with Dougie throwing his money around. "I don't know one brandy from another," said Dougie in all innocence. Out in the field Tony was no miser with the brandy, even if it did break the bank, and you had a generous tot in your coffee when you came on duty. It was strange how quickly the brandy depleted when Dougie was on duty. He didn't know one brandy from another indeed!

Corporal Martin Lyons joined our little band from one of the rifle companies and soon we would be joined by Corporal 'Bimbo' Bimbaslar, an NCO from the Pay Corps. Together we would train for our roles in

Northern Ireland. When I first went there it was 1972, the worst year for the Army in the province. This time we would be going to South Armagh, AKA Bandit Country, the most dangerous region. Apart from the usual soldierly things we had to train in, we also had to train in collating and disseminating information, how to deal with illegal check points and do our homework on the areas of our responsibilities. My area would be Newry, a town near the border. We would be away for six months so we partied like there was no tomorrow. On one such night we drank until daylight came. Not a bad thing except that I was on duty as second-in-command of the guard. I went home, got changed into my combats and magically appeared on the square for guard mount. Sergeant Nobby Clarke was the Battalion Orderly Sergeant and it was him that made we realise that I probably wasn't at my best. He stood in front of me on the inspection and started swaying side to side and I soon realised he was just matching my own sway. He never said anything, he didn't have to. Then, after inspecting the guard he marched to one side with the duty Officer and gave his command. "Guard Commander! Take post!" Except he never said that. He told me years later that he used to shout "Guard Commander! Make toast!" and nobody noticed. We marched off to the guardroom to commence our duties and the guard commander decided he would take the first watch. That cheered me up, it meant I could go in the back and get my head down for a few hours. But I'd only just drifted off when we had a power cut which wouldn't normally have bothered me but the armoury alarms all went off. More bells than Quasimodo could handle. Even so I still managed to survive the next few hours, somehow.

Chapter 19 Bandit Country

March 1979

Bessbrook was a town in South Armagh where an old imposing mill stood. This would be home to TAC HQ and C Company and we secret squirrels had an office in the restricted area along with the operations room and the Signals. This would be our home for the next six months and my last tour of Northern Ireland. Our battalion was responsible for the areas of Forkhill, Newtownhamilton, Crossmaglen and Newry. I had the Newry area while Bimbo had Newtownhamilton, Dougie had Crossmaglen and Martin had Forkhill. Ivan played in the darkroom. Because the Battalion was under strength we had The Light Infantry in Newry and my job was to liaise with them. Captain Mills was our boss (IO) and Tony Gittins was the office manager. We also shared our small office with BIT and WIS (Bomb Intelligence and Weapons Intelligence). Our bomb Int man was code named 'Hobbit' because he was a big Tolkien fan, and his office was smaller than ours and he barely had space for his table, filing cabinet and telephone. They managed to squeeze a waste paper basket in there but if he needed anything else it would require an extension being built. When Ivan told him that I had worked with explosives my life became hell. He urgently called me into his broom cupboard one day where I found him, seemingly, sounding in desperate conversation with someone on the phone. He covered the mouthpiece and indicated his filing cabinet. He asked me to get a particular file out and resumed with his highly important conversation. I opened the cabinet, pulled out the requested file and BANG! He'd booby trapped it with a small electric match, only a small bang but it makes you jump when you're not expecting it. He put the phone down and laughed his nuts off. That's OK, if he wanted to play then so could I.

Every now and again we were expected to spend time in our respective areas, which is why Bimbo was at Newtownhamilton one day. He was quite happily ensconced in the canteen when a mortar attack began on the base. Unlike the mortar attack a few years earlier in Belfast these were on target so Bimbo, along with other troops in there, scrambled under the tables. Sadly one of the men was caught out in the open with nowhere to shelter and was killed outright when a mortar hit a Land

Rover. The soldier was Private Woolmore and it was 19th March 1979. It later transpired that, a few days before the attack, people posing as council workers were taking measurements around the camp. Not long after that a flatbed lorry was parked over the road. This was their mortar base. Dougie was absolutely livid; the same tactics had been employed in his area of Crossmaglen prior to our tour. If this information was fed through to us he could have warned them and perhaps saved a life.

Later that day I was in the Operations Room where the CO and his fellow officers were discussing the incident. One of the mortar shells missed its target and hit a nearby hotel and an old lady got blown out of her bed. She wasn't seriously injured but the CO thought a goodwill visit would be nice. The 2i/c suggested a bouquet of flowers. "Bloody marvellous idea!" declared the CO. Then, just as they were deliberating over this plan, a report came in; one of our soldiers had accidentally fired his weapon in the sentry box and the errant round had hit a local taking two of his fingers off. "Damn!" exclaimed the CO, "Here we are talking about a goodwill visit and now we've shot the fingers off a local! Now what!?" Someone suggested buying him a pair of mittens. It may have been me because I remember I got chucked out of the meeting.

Sitting in the office one night I found a quiet period where I could wreak revenge on my friend the Hobbit. I wasn't short of contacts and I had in my possession an electric match! Hobbit had a desk or, to be more precise, a trestle table with an army blanket on it. I carefully drilled a very small hole through it, just below his typewriter. Then I threaded a length of fishing line through it, the top end of the line tied to his full stop key and the bottom to the switch on my booby trap. The more I thought of his face in the morning the faster my little heart beat! The trap was simple but cunning. I was still on duty when everyone else came in for their shift. The Hobbit came in and disappeared into his broom cupboard and his typewriter keys began chattering almost immediately. Chatter, chatter, chatter they went. They chattered on for an age. Does this Hobbit not use punctuation? This was no good to me; I was going off duty, so I went into his office to see what the problem was. He sat there with one hand clattering away hitting every key going while the other hand held my dismantled booby trap betwixt thumb and forefinger. "Better luck next time!" he said gleefully. I later found out there had been treachery, Ivan Jellis had been talking! The little swine had grassed me up.

Staying under the roof of the mill too long could send you nuts so Tony and I went out in the unmarked car. Not much moved around South Armagh on wheels, only us and rare supply convoys. Everything else was flown about in helicopters including the troops. This made Bessbrook the busiest heliport in Europe at the time, with Captain Maloney (MTO) running it. Taking anything out on four wheels was dangerous to say the least so we had an unmarked Fiat saloon car. To make our mode of transport safe it would be sprayed a different colour every six months and the plates changed, but when we took charge of it the thing was a bright lime green! It was almost luminous! At night you could see the eerie green glow around the corner before it came into view. That was OK though, we convinced ourselves that, with so many coats of paint, it was bullet proof. And then there was our weaponry, the 9mm Browning pistol. Blokes like Tony, stocky built with a big jacket, could happily wear a shoulder holster but me, being somewhat skinny, it looked like I was smuggling a Howitzer in my coat. In the end I had to make do with shoving it down the back of my waistband of my trousers and hoped it didn't go off. Brigade HQ was one of our destinations although we would, occasionally, visit Banbridge or Craigavon on the way. Banbridge was a small town midway between Bessbrook and Brigade HQ so when the RSM, Bill Marshall, decided that our hair was getting too long and we needed a haircut Banbridge seemed ideal. (Us secret squirrels did have hair longer than the usual regulation length but even the RSM thought there was a limit!) In Banbridge we found a barber where we could have our locks surgically snipped, then Tony suggested that we pop over to the pub. As we approached the drinking establishment Tony turned to me. "Whatever you say don't let on that you're in the Army!" he said. "It goes without saying," I told him, "Mums the word!" It wouldn't do for any careless talk so we had to be very careful. "Two pints of Guinness please," said Tony to the Barman. "What regiment are you lads with?" asked the inquisitive barman as he pulled the two beers. "3 Queen's at Bessbrook," Tony casually replied. If the barman wasn't still pouring my pint I would have choked on it! The barman plonked the two beers on the bar and took Tony's money. "There's a bit of a disco in the back room," he said, "feel free to pop in." We sauntered round to the back room. "Whatever you say don't let on that you're in the Army," I said mimicking Tony. "It's OK," said Tony, "didn't you see all the regimental plaques around the bar?" "They could have been kills!" I said. We strolled into the back room and stood at the bar, casually looking suspicious, when Tony spotted two young girls on the dance floor. "C'mon," he said, "we could be in here." We moved onto the dance floor and approached the two girls. We all jiggled about to the music and they didn't seem to mind the intrusion. The music stopped and Tony invited both of them to join us for a drink. "Fuck off yer British pig!" one said with the other nodding agreement. We'll take that as a no then. Back at the bar we both had a chat about this and that when, suddenly, I had a look of horror on may face. I shot off into the nearby gents and emerged a few minutes later. "Are you alright?" asked Tony, a little concerned. "Fine," I said, and then explained that with all that jiggling about on the dance floor it had loosened my trousers grip on my pistol. The bloody thing had fallen into the seat of my pants. I'd love to see James Bond do that when he was undercover! When we got to Brigade HQ, we mentioned this 'nice little pub' in Banbridge. They mentioned that we should avoid it really, they were pro Army but they were also number one on the IRA hit list! What a shame, just when we were getting on so well with the girls there...

"Grab your weapon John!"

I spent another night on duty in the office and I was probably drawing cartoons or plotting against the Hobbit when we received a contact report, one of our patrols had come under fire. I dropped everything and listened in to the radio net. After the initial report, the patrol sent a zap number meaning someone had been injured. (Every soldier had his own zap number so that, in the event of being injured, only his number would be sent over the air waves and not his name.) I went straight to the list, checked through the numbers and found it was Corporal Budgie Avery. But that couldn't have been right because it was Budgie on the radio. I thought maybe he'd made a mistake in the panic but no, it was indeed Budgie. He got shot in the groin but to hear him over the radio you would never have believed it. I found that incredible. I'm glad to say that he survived his wound although it probably changed his life forever.

A soldier gets his jollies in many ways and I was thumbing through a discarded girlie magazine when I came across an explicit photo of genitalia of the female variety. I got hold of Ivan (the little turncoat owed me a favour) and dragged him to his darkroom. Under my guidance he took a picture of the aforementioned naughty bits and pasted it into one of our 'most wanted' galleries. So I had a contact sheet with all these villains on it and the dirty mugshot in the middle of them. Next morning I went into Captain Mills' office clutching my sheet of mugshots. "What is it?" he asked. I showed him the sheet. "It's that one there," I said pointing to the naughty pic, "I know that twat!" It might not sound that funny but we both pissed ourselves laughing at the time. But then the IO told me that, because it had 'restricted' plastered across the top, it had to be filed! Whether he did or not I don't know but what a surprise for someone, after the 30 years, when they saw that.

Not long after that someone came into the office with grave news; my mate Jack Sear had been shot. I dashed to the heliport but, although I ran my heart out, I only manage to catch a glimpse of the chopper as it flew him off to Musgrave Hospital. It became obvious to everyone in the office that I was most concerned about my old drinking partner being shot but Captain Mills assured me that I would be going out on the next run and could take a detour. Within a few days I found myself walking down those familiar corridors of Musgrave looking for Jack. What do you say to a mate who's been shot? What state would he be in? I found Jack in his bed and I needn't have worried, he was sitting up and grinning at me. "Look!" he said, pointing at the TV in the corner, "Colour!" The big sap! He told me he had been searching a vehicle when his partner's pistol went off. Luckily the 9mm round passed through his calf muscle without hitting any bone so Jack wouldn't be departing this world any time soon. But then he told me that he was flying home the next day. Ain't life a bummer, I came here to console Jack and now I needed consolation. But at least I knew he was OK.

A few days later, back in Bessbrook, a Brigadier appeared in our office. Well, he didn't just 'appear', the visit was expected which is why we were all looking terribly busy bashing our typewriters. I don't know about the others but I was frantically typing rubbish in the hope that the Brigadier didn't come to see. The senior officer was chatting away to the IO when, suddenly, a huge blast rocked the building. The building shook that much that ceiling tiles fell about our ears. The Brigadier continued uninterrupted while the rest of us stopped typing and waited for the second explosion. Bimbo, no stranger to mortar attacks, was under his desk. There was no second blast so Bimbo crawled out of his improvised bunker and we went to see what the noise was all about. I suspected a car bomb at the gates but I was wrong. What we heard was a 1,000 lb culvert mine being set off a mile away. The RUC lost several of their number that day.

I spent another night on watch in the office and I was rather hoping for a quiet one. The first few hours were but then we had a report of two soldiers hijacking a local man's car. Soldiers? Surely not. It was most likely the IRA as usual. But, like every other unit in the area, we had to do a bed check and account for everyone. HQ Company checked in as all in order and we awaited the same from C Company. Their NCO reported back. "Two men missing," he said. Oh shit. For some odd reason these two had taken it into their heads to steal a car and head South of the border. I'll never know why because we never saw them again after the RUC nicked them. Life was never dull in South Armagh.

Bimbo, the mortar magnet, wrote a letter to a paper in Brighton pleading for pen friends. Soldiers often did this sort of thing so that they could chat up girls from the comfort of their own battlefields. I had a mate going on R&R to Brighton in the next few days so I could see us having a laugh at Bimbo's expense. I invented a girl from Brighton who would write to him. Well, I didn't exactly invent her; she already existed on a file in my cabinet! So I wrote a letter to Bimbo, from her, and described her right down to the last detail in the file, even telling him that she 'used to live in Newry'. She even gave the address! I did spice it up a bit, just enough for the envelope to steam open on its own. My mate went off to Brighton and kindly posted the letter which came back to the office. Bimbo was over the moon, his face a picture of perverted lust as he read my missive. After slobbering down the front of his army issue pullover he reluctantly let us have a read. 'She' said what she would like to do to him, naughty things which blew his hormones out of his ears. 'She' also said she used to live in Newry! "I'll check that Bimbo," I said, but Bimbo wasn't really listening, his brain was otherwise engaged. Well what a surprise when I found that file. Unbelievable. I showed it to Bimbo but he thought it was just a coincidence! That was supposed to be the end

Bimbo with yet another letter from the love of his life!

of that little jape but I could see me getting some more mileage out of it.

In the meantime I had to go and visit my Light Infantry friends in Newry. I had all the kit to patrol in, except a flak vest so I went along to the stores to see Corporal 'Granny' Goodacre, our friendly neighbourhood storeman. "What are you fackin' after?" For Granny that was quite civilised, he's normally rude. "I've come for a flak jacket," I told him. "Fack orf!" he replied, "you'll get fackin' bullet 'oles in it!" "Can I have yours then? Because you never go out anywhere." "Fack orf!!" he said and slammed the shutters down. So I got to Newry minus a flak jacket, but that didn't matter much because I'd replace one of the soldiers on the patrol and borrow his. He got the night off. "Want me boots too?" he asked, funny bleeder.

"Issue Int Section wiv a flak jacket??
You'll get it full of bullet holes!"

We patrolled the streets and pubs looking for known terrorists and intelligence. It was nice going through the bars, we were very sociable. "Alright Seamus? How's the wife? Is the beer OK?" They all totally ignored us of course. They were far chattier in Banbridge! Several times we stopped known players. I won't mention their names here but they were high profile. We would talk to them and they would talk to us, it was all very surreal passing the time with bombers and gunmen. You can have all the information in the world on these people but, by the end of the day, you needed solid evidence. Another player was spotted at the top of some steps on a footpath. The Light Infantry Int operative went and spoke to him then returned to the patrol. "That was…" but before he could finish I told him exactly who it was. "How could you know that?" he asked, "You could only see the back of his head." "Because I've done my homework," I told him. Indeed I had.

Back at Bessbrook I had to intercept Bimbo's letter to Brighton, it wouldn't do for my mate's mum to read what he wrote! But I read it, and then I wrote a reply. The letter was put in an envelope addressed to Bimbo then placed in another one addressed to my mates' mum. When she received it, she would post Bimbo's letter back.

I was in the camp cinema one night with Martin Lyons when Mick Jeng, PTI and COs bodyguard, came looking for us. He wanted to meet someone at Aldergrove Airport and needed an escort, could we help him out? The film wasn't that good so we drew out our weapons and ammunition and met him in the yard with the green Fiat. In Belfast, Mick picked up his friend and drove off leaving me and Martin in the doorway of a Chinese restaurant. It wasn't a situation I was too comfortable with; two of us in the middle of Belfast, no radio, not a soul in the British Army knowing we were there and a Browning pistol each. We went into the restaurant and, as we opened the door, a young lad ran out. It was clear that he didn't want to pay his bill. This thought was reinforced by the sight of the Chinese manager running up the aisle swearing his head off in Mandarin. As far as I was concerned it was nothing to do with us, it was between the manager and his escaping customer. That's when I saw Martins pistol appear over my shoulder. "Stop!" shouted Martin, "Stop or I'll fire!" Three things crossed my mind. Firstly, if Martin fired his pistol so close to my ear I would probably be deaf for the rest of my life.

Secondly, I didn't remember seeing anything in the 'yellow card' about shooting people because they didn't settle their restaurant bill. And thirdly, now the whole of Belfast knew we were plain clothed soldiers! I was somewhat relieved when he put his gun away, so we went in and sat down at the far end, facing the door. I could only imagine that being full of bullet holes would only serve to upset our appetites. Nobody in balaclavas came bursting in and Mick Jeng eventually returned. Then we all drove off for the safety of Bandit Country...

In Bessbrook, Bimbo was drooling over yet another letter from the love of his life. Boy was she hot, and I should know. Letters shot back and forth. Bimbo told her when he was going on leave. She said she would be on holiday too! Bimbo suggested he should meet her in Brighton. She said she would love to meet him but she was going to the Outer Hebrides! In the end we had to call a halt to this charade before we missed one of his outgoing letters. If my mate's mum got hold of one his letters she would have had a seizure. I paid a visit to my Signal friends and handed them a message that I wanted printing off from Brighton Special branch. They typed it into the teleprinter, switched it to local and printed it off. I told the IO about our cruel joke and gave him the printed message. After he read it he asked me to fetch Bimbo. I found him in the canteen. "The IO wants to see you," I told him, "and he doesn't look happy." As we walked back to the office I happened to mention that he'd also received a signal from Special Branch in Brighton. "I don't know if that's anything to do with it though," I said. Poor Bimbo, I'd never seen an Indian go pale before. Bimbo marched into the IOs office and the Captain played his part extraordinary well, we all thought he was going to have Bimbo shot before revealing the joke. But in the end the IO told him the truth about the woman of his dreams. Bimbo flew out of the office and made a bee line for me. "You rotten bastard Russell!" he screeched. Blimey, don't blame me, it was only my idea.

It was clear that the Captain was very impressed with my shenanigans because he called me into the office and told me I was now promoted to Corporal Russell. I think there was probably more to that than a few letters though. But I wouldn't be celebrating that until I got back to Dover.

We were still responsible for maps in the Int Section and we had a monster of an Ordnance Survey map to put together. It was made of dozens of maps stuck together using the gym floor and then rolled up to look like a giant drain pipe. Having done that it had to be flown to Forkhill, any volunteers? There was only one because everyone knew that the IRA used Army helicopters for clay pigeon shooting. The lone volunteer was me because I just love choppers! We used the Quick Reaction Force chopper, no seats and no doors and we flew at night. It was the roughest helicopter ride I'd ever had but we didn't get shot at and it didn't put me off flying.

There was a lot we did in South Armagh and I couldn't possibly talk about it here, but we were successful in our work. After six long months we left Northern Ireland and the Battalion wouldn't go back again until 1984. But for me I wouldn't be going back, ever.

Chapter 20   Globetrotting and APCs

July 1979

Everything returned to a normal routine in Dover and, while I was on leave after N.I., my brother, Steve, had given me an Ansell's Mild beer tap sign. This took pride of place on my desk next to my drawing board and lit up when I switched it on. This made me feel at home because I drank Ansell's Mild when I was on leave. But after a while, during one of my creative moments, I took the glass out and replaced it with some card and plastic sheet. Now it said "smile" with a big grin under the lettering. Then when you switched it on it said '"now fuck off!" Tony thought it was hilarious; he was so impressed with my artistic endeavours he went and got the IO. "Go on," said Tony, "Switch it on." How could I possibly switch it on in front of the Captain? Easy really. I'm glad to say that the IO laughed. Phew!

Dougie was a stubborn soldier and that was the case when he attempted to laminate a map on his own. It was four Ordnance Survey maps stuck together and, therefore, required a large piece of sticky laminate sheet. This is best done with two people, one laying out the laminate while the other used a straight edge to keep it flat. I offered to help but Dougie was determined to do it himself, so I just sat back and watched. It went fine at first, the laminate unfurled nicely and the straight edge did its job. Then the first crease appeared. The more Dougie tried to flatten it the worse it became. In the end I could see the look of defeat slide across his face and, with the style of a Kamikaze pilot, he threw himself into the crumpled mess. He stood up and the whole cartographer's nightmare stuck to him like a battered apron. "It didn't work," he declared and wandered off to find another map.

October 1979

Exercises were always on the cards but one came along that would be a little different. I was attached to our Signals Platoon and we were off to Italy for three weeks... for a three day exercise! We travelled to France by ferry and we all had dinner in Dunkirk. I was told it was horse meat but I couldn't swear to that. Then we boarded a troop train for Italy. The Signals were always a close knit bunch but they made me feel more than welcome. I felt like a honorary scaly back. We were based in an Italian Army barracks which was an hour's drive from Venice. The exercise went smoothly and there was very little for me to do by way of NBC and troop movements so I just helped them out where I could. After the exercise we all had a day in Venice and I couldn't help but notice how grubby it looked. No doubt if they filmed another Bond movie there they would get the cleaners in. But it was a fascinating place and we enjoyed the day very much.

One afternoon we were at a loose end so a mate suggested we go into the town, have a look around and take a few beers in. While he went for a shower I laid down on my pit and waited for him, and that was when I noticed, through the window, the sky turning a bright orange. Before I could say "What the fuck was that?" there was an almighty bang and the windows blew in throwing glass all over the place. I leapt off my bed and ran into the corridor where I bumped into my mate wrapped in his towel. He'd just turned the shower on and thought he'd blown the boiler but I said no, it was something much bigger than that. We both went outside and saw, amongst other things, an Italian soldier lying on the grass squealing. A sliver of glass had shot across his arse and he wasn't happy about it. We looked up at the barrack block we were staying in and there was a huge crack running from the roof to the foundations, it was almost like the end of the building was about to fall away. Was it a terrorist attack? The Red Brigade? Or IRA maybe? It was neither; it was an explosion in a dynamite factory some miles away. Even the Peanut Platoon couldn't manage a bang that big! Then we were told that the town was out of bounds because all the windows had blown in and they were afraid of looters. That meant that me and my mate had to go further afield and ended up in a remote village drinking with the locals. They had never met the English before and couldn't speak a word of it. But that was OK because we couldn't speak Italian. Even so we got on like a house on fire and laughed our heads off. None of us knew what we were laughing at but we laughed all the same. We returned to Dover after the three weeks and spent the rest of the year on local exercises, not the same as Italy but at least we had brandy on our night duty. Only cheap stuff though, Tony wasn't falling for that one again.

March 1980

It was nice to be all snuggled up in your own bed at home but it's a little disturbing when your wife wakes you up in the middle of the night to have a baby. To be fair she was expecting so it wasn't that much of a surprise. With our second son about to make his grand entrance I ran to the phone box with my pyjamas flapping in the breeze. (No mobile phones in them days!) Pam was driven away in the ambulance while I stayed with Stuart. My next door neighbour, Sergeant Mick Turner, told me next morning that he and his wife would have taken Stuart in. So I left him with them and shot off to Buckland Hospital. By the time I got to the hospital our son, Robert, was an hour old. The nurse passed him to me and promptly buggered off. He was twice as old when I handed him back! It was 28th March 1980. With all of that panic out of the way life returned to normal, whatever normal is in the Army.

Someone decided that the Battalion would have a day where each department would set up their stall and show everyone else what they did. Being the NBC NCO I had the pleasure of running the gas chamber! It wasn't really a gas chamber, it was a 9x9 tent but it would suffice and I had more than enough CS tablets to bring tears to everyone's eyes. There was some satisfaction to be had from gassing all of my mates as they passed through my tent, but then the Drums Platoon ambled across. Sergeant Mick Turner, my good neighbour, led them. "You won't be having us take our respirators off and giving it the old name, rank and number will you?" he asked. It sounded as though he was telling me rather than asking. "Oh yes," I told him, explaining that everyone else had and "it instils confidence in your respirator." Gullible fools! One by one they entered my gloomy tent and donned their respirators. I lit the gas tablets and watched them smoulder filling the air with its grey veil. Then we all walked around to circulate the nasty stuff. I took my position at the tent flaps and invited the first soldier forwards. Mick Turner approached me with a glare in his eyes that said "You're a dead man Russell." Luckily he couldn't see my smug grin as I asked him to remove his respirator. And he did, then gave his name, rank and number and left the tent gagging for much needed fresh air. Having defibrillated the Drums Platoon I stepped outside to admire my handy work, all of them were suitably suffering. Job done. The next group of soldiers came along and I took them into my lair, lit the tablets and circulated it. Just as I was explaining the do's and don'ts, I became aware of a big hairy arm reaching over my shoulder. Both the arm and my respirator disappeared out of the tent. I then found my escape route cut off by many hands holding the tent flaps together. After coughing up my lungs and fearing death from my own gas chamber they released me, snot and phlegm draining from my face. The rotten sods. Once the tears and snot subsided I could see a grinning Sergeant Turner holding my respirator. Could that really be the same kindly neighbour who offered to babysit my son? It was clear to me he had a very dark side...

Our next posting would be Germany and that meant changing from our Airportable role to mechanised infantry, and entailed Armoured Personnel Carriers (APCs). The Int Cell only had one APC driver, Pete Gerrard, so we needed another one. For some unexplained reason they decided that I should do the course! I did explain that I only had a provisional licence and had only just started a driving cadre but that fell on deaf ears. So, with half a driving licence and unable to drive a car, I packed my scarf and mittens and went off to Borden where I would be entrusted with a 15 ton mess tin on tracks.

The first few days were spent in the classroom where we learnt things like the German Highway Code and what makes this monstrous machine stop and go. The fun really started when they allowed us to board these vehicles and drive them. Operating them was simple, two levers to steer and stop and a pedal to make it go and a gear range selector. A child could drive one of these! As long as that child could see out of the top, although that probably wasn't too important! First thing was the emergency stop. These vehicles only travelled at 32mph but, weighing in at 15 tons, they took some stopping. We would race down the parade ground towards two cones and when the instructor yelled "Halt!" we would pull the levers back hard. The vehicle would stop and tilt on its nose leaving the driver staring at the tarmac. Boy this was fun. The instructors gave a demonstration to show what kind of damage an APC could do to a run of the mill family saloon. An old banger was parked around the back of the garages and an APC steamed into view. It trundled up to the unsuspecting car and promptly drove over it, crushing it flat. The point of the lesson was to show us how careful we should be when sharing the road with the public. Then we had the nerve racking business of taking these beasts out onto the road for the first time. Although we may have frightened the motoring public at times I didn't see any crushed cars at the side of the road. When we weren't on the public roads we were driving on deserted tracks or ploughing through the woods. Either way it was hazardous.

If you weren't driving this monster you'd be standing up in the back admiring the scenery as it flashed by at 32mph. That's where I was, looking out of the back, when someone shouted "Duck!!" I should have read that as an instruction but, being nosey, I wanted to see what we were ducking for. It was a branch. A big thick branch, and it hit me right in the beret! The vehicle pulled over so I could find my beret, which I did, but my cap badge was lost forever.

When you drive one of these 'mini tanks' there are other responsibilities put on you. You need to know how to change the tracks and to teach us to do this they parked the big lump of armour on the square and took a track off. Being parked on a flat surface made the job easier, even though the tracks weighed one ton each. If it was on the training areas things could be a lot more difficult, as we were about to find out.

Sergeant Chris Rodziewicz was our instructor and he stood in the commander's cupola giving me, the driver, instructions. We came across an uphill fork on a muddy track and he ordered me to go left. I pulled on the left lever and put my foot down but the beast wanted to go right. "Left!" he shouted. "It wants to go right!!" I shouted even louder. That's because he had a mic and I didn't. Communication was very much a one way thing in these training vehicles. "Just keep pulling on the lever!" he demanded. I'm sure they told us that was a bad thing when we did the theory. But he was the boss so I pulled on the left lever and put my foot down. The engine roared, the vehicle grumbled and I saw a track going ahead of us. Oh shit. Now we'd thrown a track and to make matters worse we were up to our axles in mud. We all climbed out and went into track changing mode with mud up to our knees. But we did manage it. It was late when we got back to camp and the cookhouse was closing, but the duty cook knocked something up for us. "It was Corporal Russell's fault," said Chris, "he threw a track!" Cheers mate, rank definitely does have its privileges!

Clattering down public roads in these vehicles became quite enjoyable, an awesome experience. A lot of the time we would nip down the Petersfield Road towards Portsmouth but, luckily for the population of Portsmouth, we never went that far. I was driving that way one day and was told to take the next roundabout and head back. Unlike a car steering one of these things was a jerky affair, constantly pulling at the lever to get it round. It was so jerky that one of the lads in the back hit his head on the first aid box. I guess that was lucky!

We also had to learn the art of driving with the hatches down which left us peering through the periscope, two black rubber eye pieces. No, we didn't do this on public roads which would have been far too entertaining. We did this on the ups and downs of the training area. This was a rather claustrophobic way to drive because you could only see straight ahead and it gave you a different angle of view, especially when you went up slopes. Just when you thought you had reached the top of the slope and eased off the accelerator the bloody thing rolled back down again. Too much of that and you were in danger of rocking the soldiers to sleep in the back!

After several weeks of wrestling with these vehicles we were ready for our tests. As I mentioned earlier the comms in these training vehicles were a one way thing, the commander could talk to me but I couldn't talk to him, which was a shame really. First we had the emergency stop, slamming on brakes and rubbing my nose on the tarmac. Then it was out on the road. Now if I had been paying attention when the testing officer said "keep going straight on unless I tell you any different", things would have been fine. But I wasn't paying attention was I. Because of my inattentiveness I ended up driving two miles further than I needed to. Still, I passed. So now I could drive 15 tons of tracked armour but I couldn't drive a family saloon. Unless it had tracks on it.

June 1980

No sooner had we got back into the partying routine of Dover we had to sober up and fly off to Canada again. Mind you, I wasn't complaining. Sitting on the aircraft I got bored so I drew cartoons of the flight crew including the pilot. I couldn't see the pilot so I could only guess he was wearing a leather flying helmet and was sporting a fine handlebar moustache. It was all good fun, until we approached Edmonton. "The Captain wants to see you up front," said one of the cabin crew and he wasn't laughing. Oh shit, I enjoyed flying up until that moment. I was frogmarched to the cockpit where the Captain was and, surprisingly, he wasn't wearing a leather flying helmet and no hint of a moustache. I expected more of the RAF. They sat me in the loadmaster's seat, strapped me in and plonked headphones on my head. "This is it," I thought, "this must be the seat of torture!" But instead of electrocuting me, one of the crew handed me a manual. "See this list," he said, "When the Captain calls them out you say 'check', OK?" "What if they're not checked?" I asked. "They will be," he said and the aircraft made its approach. I heard the Captain over the headphones. "Oil pressure." "Check." "Engine temperature." "Check." "Under carriage down." "Check." I had no idea what he was on about but he spoke and I checked. Then I heard him talking to control at Edmonton where he told them we were making our final approach. Really? Surely we needed a runway for that and I couldn't see one, and believe me I could see everything from my seat. Then, in the distance, I could see it, the tiniest bit of tarmac ever. The one we had at Brize Norton was like an eight lane motorway! I'm glad to say that the closer we got the bigger the airstrip became. I told the Captain it was a wonderful experience and thanked him. When I left the cockpit some gullible soldier asked me if I landed the aircraft. I told him it was amazing what you could do with a tracked vehicle licence.

After a short drive from Edmonton we arrived in the familiar surroundings of Camp Wainwright once again. But this time there was no digging monumental shit houses or building bridges, our role was range safety for the live firing exercises. That meant that we would be spending most of our time driving around in a bright orange APC, the safety vehicle. That made a pleasant change from the usual black and olive drab. It was while we were bouncing over the plains in our orange mess tin when we had a call to attend a first aid case. On the way to the location we suspected 'hatch rash' where someone comes into contact with some unexpected piece of heavy armour. When we arrived, the casualty was sitting against the road wheels and was looking white as a sheet and cradling his hand. On closer inspection it appeared he had almost severed the fingers of his hand. This was a bad case of hatch rash. The helicopter was called, arrived and flew him off for treatment with his mates calling behind him. "Can I have your gloves!!?" Such poor taste. I'd have had his pen.

At other times we would be doing safety on the firing ranges, a range which was only a short walk from our base camp but took us behind a battery of artillery guns. That was OK as long as we did walk behind them and not in front! Safety was crucial on the live firing range and you had to be very aware of everything and anything that was going on, especially when the troops moved down the range. The firing started from a line of trenches and I was with one of the soldiers who appeared to have difficulty seeing the target come up. Every time it popped up he couldn't see it, so I pointed it out to him. "See it now?" I asked. "Got it Corporal!" he replied. "So what are you going to do now?" I asked him. With the confidence of a future leader he called out to the other trenches. "Target to my front! Watch my tracer!" Very impressive. Then he fired two shots at the target, neither one a tracer round. "What happened to the tracer?" I asked him. "I ain't got any Corporal," he said. I looked down at him in his trench. "So what was all that 'watch my tracer' business then?" "Well," he said, "That's what they all say ain't it." I've gave him 5 out of 10 for initiative, 10 out of 10 for being a tit.

Then the soldiers would move from their trenches and start the battle run. Not a bad thing but they were firing live rounds and depended on us, the range safety staff, to ensure nobody got killed. You would have the group in the centre and groups on the left and right flank, all going down the range firing their lethal weapons. If, as range safety, you went with the group left flanking then you would stand up on the right of them, in full view so that the safety staff behind you could see where they were, then they would make sure you didn't come into their group's arc of fire. To make us stand out from the firing crowd we wore white armbands because, they told me, they made us bullet proof. (If that's true why didn't we all wear them in Northern Ireland?) The responsibility of having so many soldiers depend on you was frightening really. But we managed to get the troops through without getting anyone killed so we must have been doing something right.

There are times in between companies firing where we had a chance to slip back to our base camp for a brew. Having had a cup of coffee me and my mate made our way back to the range, chatting as we went. We were still chatting idly away when we passed the mighty guns of the artillery, like we had done so many times before. But unlike before the guns exploded into life! The first one fired and the ground shook nearly putting us on our arses! By the time we got to the end of the path we were both suffering shell shock. Noisy sods.

With the live firing exercises over with, we were all rewarded with some welcome R&R. Tony decided we would hire a car, a huge Chrysler Impala, and we would drive off to nowhere in particular. We thought if we were driving then we should at least have a destination so we chose Saskatoon in neighbouring Saskatchewan; we just didn't get that far. We first stopped off at some outpost where we had a beer and met the nicest of girls. One of them told us that her dad was a Drum Major in the Scots Guards. Better behave ourselves here then! And we did, apart from lying with my head in her lap while she fed me grapes. Oh, and we also nearly went skinny dipping at the local open air pool but everyone else in Canada decided they would too so we cancelled that. We would have preferred a bit of privacy. But we generally behaved ourselves and the following morning we said goodbye to the girls and headed off to Saskatoon once again. Except we never got that far.

We pulled up at a bar in Lone Rock, a small place just across the border in Saskatchewan, and went in for some light refreshment. Failing that beer would do. When we ordered our beer the barman asked if we were English. We said we were and he said that Molly would love to meet us. "That's fine," we said, having no idea who Molly was, "Where is she?" "Sitting round the corner with her husband," he replied. So we went round the corner and found Norman and Molly Clark, a lovely couple. Molly came from England but she met Norman when he was stationed there during the war with the Canadian Air Force. They both got married and she'd lived with him here ever since. Norman asked where we were staying. "I'm sleeping in the trunk of the car because there's plenty of room to stretch out in there," I told him. "No," said Norman, "You can all stay at our small ranch." We tried not to impose on them but they were both insistent so we followed them back to their 'small' ranch. We got there as the sun was setting and they were a very hospitable family. We had a chat and a few more beers then they showed us the bunks in the basement, our sleeping quarters. After some more beers we bade them goodnight and turned in. In the meantime their son and daughters arrived home and Molly must have told them about 'the English guests'. We know that because we would hear footsteps coming down the stairs followed by a meek 'Hello?' "Hello." We would reply in our unmistakable English accents. Then they ran up the steps giggling. Clearly they had never heard the English before.

In the morning we had a superb breakfast and Norman asked me what I wanted to do. "I've always fancied myself as a cowboy," I told him. No sooner had I said it than he had his son drive me across their small ranch to the barn. Small ranch? It took us 45 minutes to get there - in a pick-up truck! I can't recall the name of their son but he introduced me to a horse, a horse with one eye and the girth of a beer barrel.

"STOP! WHOA! HEEL!"

First he got me to ride it around the outside of the barn, gently coaxing it round the corners by pulling on the reins. Bear in mind that I had no saddle or stirrups and the reins were two separate pieces, not a loop. Nothing like the westerns at all. Not even a saddle bag or Winchester! This short tutorial went fine until I came across a spar sticking out of the barn wall. My first instinct was to raise my hands to stop the thick wooden pole hitting me in the face. But to do that I'd dropped the reins, the reins I needed to stop the horse. Without any control he would just carry on, and that's exactly what it did, it plodded on leaving me clinging, horseless, to a spar. The lad cracked up. "I've only ever seen things like that in the movies!" he said. It's a shame he didn't have a camera then. Then young Master Clark took his steed out into the open fields with me following at a steady trot. A nice steady ride until he shouted "Yee-ah!" and bolted off at a gallop. I didn't say anything to my horse but he twisted his head so he could see with his good eye and decided to join the fun. The bloody horse raced off at a gallop with me clinging to its mane and my arse sliding sideways! Back at the ranch I strolled in with my new bow legs. "Feel like a cowboy now?" asked Norman. "Oh yes," I said. Norman laughed his head off. "I can tell by the horse shit on your arse!" he said and laughed some more. It could have been horse shit. After that ride it could have been mine.

Brian Cunliffe was there but he was more happy playing with the tractor than riding one eyed horses. Not a normal tractor, this was a Massey Ferguson and was the size of a house with stereo radio and air conditioning. It was most likely built in Coventry across the road from my school. That afternoon we fired a .22 Winchester at some gophers just to round things off. Then we said our sad farewells and left for Wainwright. They were a wonderful family and I'll never forget them. Thanks Norman and Molly for a great time.

After a little more range safety at Wainwright we prepared to move back to Dover. But this time we didn't have a VC10, we would be flying back in a Hercules cargo plane! What a flight that was, one chemical toilet between us and all of us sitting in canvas seats with bundles of cotton wool sticking out of our ears. When we landed at Brize Norton we were all profoundly deaf!

The rest of our time in Dover was spent on exercises training for our mechanised role in Germany. Meanwhile the RQMS, Mickey Wishhussen, was now the RSM. My mate Corporal Bob 'Jonah' Jones will testify to that. Jonah was a likeable bloke (and still is!) and he happened to be guard commander one day. For some reason it was his first and only duty as Guard Commander. He stamped into the RSMs office, received his orders and a nice crisp guard commander's report to fill in during the course of that duty. Jonah had never filled one in before so his first effort was a bit of a cock up. But that was OK, with some help and three reports later he had one he was proud of. He came off duty the next morning and proudly presented his report to the RSM. Micky Wish studied it and looked at Jonah. "This isn't the report I gave you," he said. Jonah insisted it was. "No it's not," said the RSM, "Look!" He held it up to the light. Apparently sneaky Mickey had put two pin holes in the corner of the report he had given him. Jonah's biggest worry was getting extra duties but the RSM was obviously impressed with Jonah. No action taken.

But now it was time to prepare for the move to Germany. We said our goodbyes to all the civilian friends we had made in Dover and handed over the new quarter which had been our home in Burgoyne Heights. Then we flew off with our wives and children to a new home in Fallingbostel, West Germany where we would fight the cold war. And it really was cold!

Chapter 21 Fallingbostel

April 1981

Fallingbostel was a small town south of Hamburg and north of Hannover and our flat was on the Heidemark Estate just outside the town. The Battalion was now posted to St. Barbara Barracks which was a thirty minute walk away. On the estate we were close to new and old neighbours so that made it very cosy. What we didn't have was a TV. (The one we had in Dover was hired so we couldn't really take that!) We paid a visit to SKC and purchased a Panasonic black and white TV with cassette player and radio. The screen was about 7 inches and we had to sit on top of it to see it. One thing we grew fond of was sausages, bockfurst or curryfurst, it didn't really matter. The camp was an old Wehrmacht barracks full of grand buildings and basements galore. (Even our block of flats had basements, or maybe they were bunkers?) HQ Company had its own basement and that's where I found my new, but temporary, office. That's how proud of me they were, tucking me away in a basement like some deformed relative they didn't like to speak of! One of the outgoing NCOs showed me around the Int setup. "Look in here," he said and led me into a room dominated by a huge tiled slab, raised like a shower base with drainage holes. "Crazy golf?" I asked my guide. "Nah," he replied. "This is where they did autopsies during the war!" Well that was comforting being opposite my office. I then gave my guide the slip before he came out with any more gems.

Exercises were more frequent now, it seemed like we were taking our APCs out every other week. But in the Int Section we were somewhat more comfortable than the average soldier and we were near the top of the food chain. We were always with TAC HQ in the field, sharing the outdoor life with the likes of the CO and the RSM. (The RSM was still Mickey Wish.) More often than not we would drive into our 'hide' and one of the Regimental Policemen would guide our vehicles in position, usually Rasher Rigden or Jock McKeown. But one day I drove into our location and had the pleasure of the RSM guiding me in. He stood to the front of the vehicle and, with some hand waving, had me reversing the vehicle under some trees. As I reversed I couldn't help but notice the smile on his face, maybe he was thinking of Jonah's guard commander's report, I don't know. I returned the smile, but only a quick one, I didn't want to appear too familiar. He continued to look strangely satisfied as he waved me backwards. Then a thick branch hit me in the back of the head! The RSM wandered off, laughing like a drain, while I recovered my beret from out of the foot well. I can laugh about it now though, the swelling's gone down.

Not having a car of my own, or even a full licence for that matter, I had to walk into camp. One morning I only just made it for muster parade, a close call because the RSM was taking it. (It wouldn't do to have him laughing while he locked me up!) We formed up in three ranks and Mickey Wish began his inspection, which went fine until he got to me. "Why are you wearing a combat jacket Corporal Russell?" he asked. I told him I had walked into camp from my quarter and it was a tad chilly. "Part one orders state summer dress!" he shouted, "Get the jacket off!" That was a bit of a problem because we soldiers had the habit of cutting our shirt sleeves down which made them easier to roll up and iron. My sleeves were cut down and weren't rolled up. If the RSM saw that he would consider it a case of defacing Army equipment and invite me to the guardroom. I slowly began to unbutton my jacket and, when I felt he was a safe distance along the ranks, I quickly removed it and rolled my sleeves up. He came to my rear and seemed satisfied. Phew! But there was someone in the rear rank who wasn't so lucky and he was also wearing his combat jacket.

"Well Sir, I think I can explain ..."

"Get it off!" demanded the RSM. "I can't Sir," replied the hapless soldier, "I haven't got a shirt on Sir." "So what's this then?" enquired the RSM tugging at his collar. "Just a shirt collar Sir," replied the doomed squaddie. Unlike me and my sleeves he had cut up his shirt leaving just the collar and buttoned front. Needless to say the soldier was doubled off to the guardroom after which he was escorted to the QMs clothing store to purchase a new shirt. When it comes to defacing Army equipment there is a limit!

Because we were stationed so close to the border we were in a constant state of readiness and a 'stand to' would be held with frenzied frequency. We would all parade with our kit and vehicles and the top brass would carry out an inspection to satisfy themselves that we were indeed ready. The fact that we were warned beforehand had nothing to do with it. Many a night I would lie on my bed in full kit and wait for the knock on the door. When the knock came we would climb aboard the waiting truck and get transported to the camp. After an inspection and a few administrative things we would be back home for breakfast. That's how it usually happened. One night, after the usual tip off, I was on my bed in full kit and waited for the call. When we got to the camp we had the usual kit inspection and climbed aboard our vehicles waiting to be dismissed. But we weren't dismissed, we were ordered to drive out of camp. Worse than that we drove for miles and hid in a wood, all before daybreak! Poor Pam had the breakfast on and she wouldn't see me for two weeks! If that wasn't bad enough I only had ten fags on me. A fortnight later I turned up at the flat with the remains of camouflage cream on my shirt collar and smelling like something horrible. "You're not coming in here like that!" Pam said. So I stripped off on the doorstep before she would let me in. It wasn't that she was house proud; she just didn't want me taking the edge off her air freshener.

On another planned exercise we raced out of camp at 32mph and hid ourselves in the woods at a secret location. One by one the APCs drove into the secret area... followed by a green and white police car. Apparently we passed a road works and the last vehicle had caught some pickets dragging those and the red and white tape all the way to our location. Herr Policeman thought it would be a nice gesture if we gave it back. You could always tell where these vehicles had been by the tell-tale teeth marks in the kerb stones where our tracks had come too close. That's probably why we moved mostly at night, otherwise we would be dragging shoppers off to our secret places.

Captain Rayner was the IO now and on one exercise I was driving and he was in the commander's cupola. We drove the vehicle into a farmyard and parked up so the IO could get his bearings. That was when Herr Farmer came marching out of his house with a pitchfork. Although we couldn't understand a word he said we could only guess by his hysterical tone that he wasn't inviting us in to share his breakfast sausage. Captain Rayner, still in the early stages of his German language course, couldn't make head nor tail of his ranting either. After receiving a lot of Germanic abuse the IO decided we should depart, all of this shouting was playing havoc with his map reading. We drove out of the farmyard with the farmer still blowing a gasket. "Yes, yes," said the IO cheerily, "Goodbye and fuck orf!" It later transpired that we were parked on his cattle's winterfeed. Apparently they get funny about that sort of thing.

The next day I sat in the wagon and decided to roll a fag. Having ran out of cigarettes before I decided roll ups were the way to go. The baccy did go further but I'd run out of rolly papers!

Ration pack loo paper is never a substitute for roll up papers

After a brief spell of panic I regained my sense of resourcefulness and dived into one of the ration packs. The toilet paper issued with these packs were squares of paper, one grade down from grease proof paper, but somewhat bigger than your average roll up paper. Obviously it didn't have a gummed edge so I had to liberally slobber over it to stop it from unfurling. Then I lit it. The first two puffs were OK but then it started to dry out and unfold. So I tilted my head and pointed the disintegrating cigarette into the air in the hope of getting at least one more drag out of it. At that point an Officer happened to pass by and looked in. It took me ages to convince him that it wasn't a reefer I was smoking.

Being the Battalion NBC NCO definitely had its advantages. It made me head and shoulders above mere mortals when it came to all things toxic. We were on one exercise when our position came under chemical attack. Not a real chemical of course, you can't leave that stuff lying about on the training areas. It was bad enough burying our turds all over the place. No, this was part of the exercise. We in the Int Section sat in the rear of our closed down vehicle, puffing away on a cigarette and working out our wind directions and plotting the hazards. Then Rasher Rigden, Regimental Police, turned up in his respirator and peered through the thick glass spy hole. "Respirators!" he shouted through his rubber face, "Why aren't you wearing respirators?!" "Not required," I shouted back, "we're battened down with the air filtration on!" Rasher waddled off apparently happy with my expert explanation. If he had looked closer he would have seen that our top cover was open to let the cigarette smoke out.

Somewhere along the way we acquired a new 'temporary' IO, a young Lieutenant fresh from Sandhurst. He sat in the back of our vehicle with us on day one of an exercise. "What happens now then Corporal Russell?" he asked after settling into our location. "Now Sir, we wait." I told him, "Most of this job is about waiting Sir." Safe in the knowledge that he was in the hands of an experienced NCO he sat back and waited. After two or three days he began to get restless, as Officers are prone to do, and wandered off to a briefing. It wasn't long before he returned. "I think you have been economical with the truth Corporal," he said to me. "What could you possibly mean Sir?" I asked, having been taken aback with such a slur on my good character. The truth is the rest of us had been doing what was necessary during the last few days so we hadn't really wangled an easy life. To be fair he laughed it off and put it down to experience. I just wish I could recall his name...

The Ops Officer was a wonderful man and I do recall his name, Captain Guy Waller. For operational reasons our vehicles would be parked back to back with a tent, known as a penthouse, thrown across. In the dead of night we could happily chat across to each other, a cosy arrangement that came in very handy because one night he called across. "Draw some cartoons Russ," he pleaded. I told him it wasn't possible because although I had the pens and plenty of paper I had no cigarettes, and no cigarettes equalled no inspiration. "You draw," said the Captain, "and I'll supply the fags." That sounded like a fair plan so all night long cartoons and smokes passed between us. Come the morning the Captain would take his usual shower, achieved by having one of his men standing on the vehicle and pouring a jerry can of water over his head. He did miss his home comforts.

At about this time Tony Gittins left us, retiring to Malta where his wife, Sonia, came from. Joining us was WOII John O'Sullivan, a fairly laid back man but the shit would hit the fan if he spotted my white socks peeking over the top of my puttees. But without Tony who would bring the brandy on exercise? It wasn't to happen again.

Life in Fallingbostel did have its drawbacks, you really needed a car to get away from the place and see anything. So I went to our ever helpful NAAFI and bought one, a brand new Datsun Bluebird estate. All I needed now was a licence! But at least I could drive into work with Corporal Ernie Ainsworth at my side and fahrschule plates on my car. Ernie proved invaluable when he came to teaching me the finer points of driving. Ernie spent months teaching me to drive which he did very well. He didn't lose too much hair and he kept his panic attacks to a minimum. One day he told me that I was ready to take my test, probably told to say that by his doctor, so I booked myself in with the testing officer from the Royal Hussars. Due to the amount of snow on the ground he decided we would forego the emergency stop. "If you slam the brakes on the bloody car won't stop until we get to Hamburg!" he said. So off we went, taking the driving test in the snow. But I passed and now me and the family had a new found freedom. It also saved me the cost of converting the car to tracks.

We became great friends with Sergeant Nobby Clarke and his wife Pat, but they lived on the other side of Fallingbostel on the Interbau Estate. This would normally involve a long trek or a taxi ride to see them but now we could just jump in the car. That was much better except that one weekend we were warned to stay away from the town because the Nazi Party were having a rally. Yes, even then there were followers of the Nazis and they didn't think much of us British being in their country. That wasn't a problem for us, we'd just take a detour round the range road. Having spent a lovely afternoon with Brian and Pat we packed our two children into the car and headed back to the Heidemark Estate. It was evening and the rally should have been over at 6 o'clock so we could cut though the town. What a mistake that was. We drove into the town and went through the main street and as we approached the main junction I noticed vehicles being stopped by someone wearing a balaclava and carrying a pickaxe handle. Then others appeared. The more I saw, the less I liked it. They were obviously the Nazi thugs that had held their rally earlier and I'm sitting with my family in a car with BFG plates! That might have made it a little difficult convincing them I was a local! Without another thought I put the car in reverse and swerved into a side street, blue smoke coming from the tyres. Luckily there were no cars behind although one of the thugs came close as he ran out of a bar. To be honest, if I had hit him I wouldn't have stopped because these people meant business. That night we watched the news on TV and BFG registered vehicles had been turned over and torched. A close call indeed, I didn't mind a bit of adventure but that was frightening.

The winter was now taking a tight grip on Germany and it really was cold. But the exercises still went on. One exercise took us thirty miles down the autobahn. This required special permission from the local burghers because a convoy of lumbering 15 ton boxes travelling at 32mph wasn't what the German public were used to on their motorways. But it was freezing and, even though I was wearing combat gloves, my hands were like blocks of ice. Because I'd lost all feeling in my hands I had to pull the levers with my forearms. When we arrived in our location we had to camouflage the vehicle and dig a trench. The first thing I did was put my hands against the engine louvres to thaw out my frozen digits. Shit! But that hurt! Indescribable pain. We did camouflage the vehicle but trying to dig a trench when I couldn't grip the shovel was something else. It was hours before I got any sensation back into my hands and that would be a problem that would plague me for the rest of my life. But only when it was cold.

I found the lecture theatre much warmer and that's where I held my NBC lessons. It wasn't all about gassing people! It was bewildering standing up in front of fifty soldiers and taking a lesson, like a stand-up comedian armed only with a book of crap jokes. But I got the lesson across which was the object of the exercise. Urination and defecation drills were a favourite. Firstly undo the cloth braces holding up your NBC trousers and tie them together in a bow. Don't tie a knot! Then undo your trousers and ease down your NBC trousers and your combat trousers until you feel the tied bow under your chin. Then crouch down

"Go directly to jail, do not pass go, do not collect 200 pounds!"

(Jock McKeown, Regimental Policeman)

and go about your business. If the cloth braces start to strangle you then you've just shit in your pants, you should have pulled them to one side. Then I would take them through the decontamination drills and getting their pants back up. Having taught them that I had a bit of useful advice; forget all of that, wear bicycle clips and shit your pants. It was the safest bet.

One day I had a lecture planned and drove into the camp but ended up in a tail back. The Regimental police decided to have a vehicle documents check at the gate and a queue of traffic formed. I would happily have sat there but I knew my documents were not up to date and that could cause some hassle. So I turned off towards the lecture theatre. Jock McKeown stopped me. "Documents check," he said, "you should be in the line." I looked at him through the window. "But I have to set up for an NBC lecture," I said. "It doesn't matter," he said, "nobody is exempt!" "OK, but the 2i/c and the CO have ordered this lecture," I lied, "Can you call the 2i/c and tell him why I'm late?" Jock kindly waved me through. "When you've done that make sure you come through the check point." I then spent an hour at the lecture theatre until the Regimental Police got fed up and went back to do whatever they did. Once I got back onto the camp I updated my documents.

OK, I said it wasn't all about gassing people but sometimes we would. We didn't have a gas chamber but they had one in the Hussars camp. A proper brick built chamber where we could gas people properly! Myself and two aides went over there one day with a bucket full of CS tablets. We had hundreds of soldiers passing through our gas chamber, we also gassed ourselves. Not in the chamber but in the car on the way back. Having spent hours in the chamber the gas had built up in our jackets. Not very noticeable out in the open but when the three of us got in the car to drive back the vehicle seemed to fill up with gas. So we opened the windows and probably gassed everyone we passed too. It's terrible driving when you've got tears in your eyes.

Having access to CS gas tablets almost got me into trouble. A Sergeant approached me in my office. "Give us a couple of CS tablets," he said like a junkie asking for a fix. "What!" I said, "They're classed as ammunition." "I only want a couple," he said. Would he ask the ammo storeman for a couple of bullets?! Of course not. "Do you think I keep them in my drawer or something?" I said. But he was most persuasive so I reached into my drawer and gave him two. Why would he want two CS tablets? He told me there was the most annoying Sergeant in the mess and he noticed that he put his electric bar heater on in his room before taking a shower. He wanted to put one of these tablets on one of the bars and let it smoulder there and wait for him to return. Anybody who knows anything about CS will tell you that being wet and gassed was a terrible thing. That's why I agreed to let him have them, because it sounded like fun! So one evening the annoying Sergeant did the usual thing, switched on his heater and went for a shower. The unnamed Sergeant crept into his room and put a tablet on each bar and legged it. Did the annoying Sergeant suffer? Yes, and so did the rest of the Sergeants Mess because the first floor of the building became a giant gas chamber! Lots of questions were asked of me the next morning but I pleaded ignorance at every turn. I would love to have seen it, although I would have worn my respirator.

April 1982

We often visited the ranges at Sennelager and that's where we were when we got wind of the Falklands. It was in all of the papers and we followed it with great interest. Then we were told that we would be returning to Fallingbostel a few days earlier than expected so rumours went all over the place about us going out there. As it happened we weren't down to go and had no involvement. At first we thought back to Guatemala and the sabre rattling in Belize but, as we now all know, that wasn't the case and war did break out. We continued with our exercises in case the Russians decided to pop over and then we were told we were off to Canada once again. Oh good, at least it was warmer out there and my digits wouldn't drop off...

Chapter 22 The Beginning of the End

Two years had passed since we last visited the vast wilderness of Canada and Camp Wainwright hadn't changed a bit. We had wonderful warm weather during the day but it got a tad cold in the night. Most nights it snowed. Whatever happened to those balmy nights where we slept under the stars? So my fingers still suffered in the low temperatures. Most of our days and nights were spent in the field, unlike some of them we had with us. They preferred their beds and hot showers. I may have been having problems with the circulation in my fingers but the lads I worked with were great and I was happy to spend time with them. But it didn't always go down well with the hierarchy.

There were days when the exercise would cease and we would have a maintenance day where the vehicles were checked over. Very wise when you consider that these vehicles would never be passed for use on the road in Blighty. They were one step away from being scrapped. Once we were happy that these machines would see us through another day we could relax. It was one of those 'relaxed' moments when I upset the Battalion 2i/c, Major Shepherd. The lads on our safety vehicle were a great bunch, they knew what had to be done and they did it without question, which made my life easier. We were having a laugh and a joke on top of our vehicle when the 2i/c came sauntering over. He looked up at us and I bade him good afternoon. "Don't you think the men should be doing something Corporal Russell?" he asked. "All the maintenance is done Sir," I told him, "The vehicle is ready to roll." Clearly he wasn't happy with that. "Perhaps you should keep the troops entertained," he said. By this he meant to carry out some background activity like map reading or other soldier like things. I knew what he meant but I thought, wrongly, that he had a sense of humour. "Actually Sir," I said, "I was thinking of breaking into a song and dance routine." Obviously I had misjudged the Major, and to prove the point he stormed off with a face like thunder and blood vessels exploding. The situation wasn't helped when the lads burst into fits of laughter. At least they found it funny. Any chance of Corporal Russell becoming Sergeant Russell was killed at that very moment.

Another night was spent in the field, at least the crew and myself spent the night there, the other senior staff decided to suffer the indignation of going back to camp for clean sheets and a shower. How they sacrificed themselves. But that was alright because the NAAFI wagon paid a visit to our location and I managed to bum a crate of beer for the lads. I used the old tried and tested 'I'll pay you on Friday' ploy which worked fine, until Friday came around! So while the rest of our team roughed it in comfy beds we lived it up with a crate of Labatt's.

"No not this Friday, next Friday!"

The exercise rolled on and we did our thing. Then another maintenance day came around. That's when a certain NCO wandered over and took me aside to a nearby tent. "The 2i/c wants me to have a word," he said. Ok I thought, wondering what that 'word' could be. "He thinks you're too friendly with the troops," he said, "they should be addressing you as 'Corporal' and not first name terms." It was true, we were a friendly bunch and I always found that if you treated soldiers like mates then you got the best out of them. If I told one of them to stick his head under the tracks while I moved forward he would say "OK John, but don't mess my hair up." And it was true, the Army didn't like that sort of thing, there was a chain of command. "Is the work getting done?" I asked him. "Well yes..." he replied. "And is the 2i/c complaining about the safety on the range?" "No but..." "Then he's got fuck all to moan about then has he!?" I said. The NCO rattled on about discipline and familiarity among the men, a fair point but I was enraged. "To be honest," I said, "I couldn't give a fuck what the 2i/c thinks as long as the job is a good one and the men are happy!" "Shh!" said the sneaky Corporal in an embellished stage-aside, "He's in the tent!" Well, I didn't see that one coming did I? The final nail in my promotion coffin was well and truly hammered home.

Me and the crew continued our unacceptable life style out in the wilderness and there comes a time when you just have to have a crap. There was no luxurious thunderbox here like the one we built so many moons ago! There weren't even any bushes to hide behind, just open plain. I wasn't desperate so I thought I'd wait until dark. Night time fell and everyone in the tent seemed to be preoccupied with beer and Russell's promotion prospects when I took a shovel and disappeared into the dark. I walked about 200 yards, dug a hole and with my trousers around my ankles I leaned on the shovel. Release at last. Then the search light came on. After a very short search it picked me out but I was already committed. All I could hear from the direction of the light was jeering. Rotten bleeders. They told me afterwards that I looked like Long John Silver with short legs!

Something strange happened one night, Major Shepherd and his 'clean sheets' cohorts spent the night with us! They even convinced the previously mentioned NCO to stay out with us. I bet he was gutted. As usual the NAAFI wagon came around and I managed to blag a crate of Labatt's beer for me and the lads courtesy of 'Friday'. Unfortunately a Captain with us, who I will refer to as 'Wanker', only managed to procure a crate of cats piss. I thought that was very fitting but Captain Wanker swapped it for our Labatt's when we weren't looking! Is that what they teach them at public school? No wonder the country is in the shit. After a few beers we turned in for the night, all huddled up in our 9x9 tent like one big happy family. Then as we nodded off the bloke next to me started snoring. Not a gentle, contented snore but a sound that echoed around the plain like a warthog in pain. It did bother me but not as much as it bothered Captain Wanker. "Shut up!" he hissed. He wouldn't shout it out for fear of waking up the 2i/c in the sleeping bag next to him. Then, when he got tired of hissing, he chucked his boot across. That didn't bother the snorer one bit because the offending footwear hit me in the back. "Hey!" I yelled, "Watch where you're throwing them boots!!" That woke the 2i/c up. "What the facks going on!?" he croaked. "Some wanker throwing boots from over there!" I replied, knowing full well it was Captain Wanker who had thrown it. Ah, where else could you get away with calling an Officer a wanker and get away with it! After that I left the two Officers to squabble between themselves. Meanwhile the snorer continued snoring totally unaware of the commotion he had caused...

At 04:00 hrs we were all rudely awakened by the 2i/c, he had decided that the company spearheading the 'attack' needed back up. So that's why the wily old dog spent the night in the field, he wanted to play soldiers! With everything packed and stacked we headed off to the front line. Major Shepherd and his mates had gone ahead while we packed and stacked so we met them down there. It was just approaching daylight when the 2i/c came over to us. He started telling us that the rifle company didn't need us when he stopped in mid-sentence. He strode over to me and rubbed my chin. "We haven't shaved this morning have we Corporal Russell?" he said. I felt like replying 'You as well Sir, when we were doing all the packing?' but I resisted because I was in enough shit already. But I had come to the conclusion that Major Shepherd had taken a serious dislike to me and catching Russell out was becoming a national sport.

After spending the day watching real soldiers shoot each other we prepared for a night move. Pete Gerrard would be driving the APC and I had the privilege of driving the Land Rover with Captain Wanker on board. "Where are we going Sir?" I asked, trying to be cordial. Well the Captain turned and looked at me like he had stepped in something odious. "Just follow the vehicle in front!" he ordered. I take it he had no idea where we were going either. Following the vehicle in front was easier said than done for two reasons. Firstly it was pitch black and we were driving on convoy lights, a small light on the back of the vehicles. Secondly the vehicle in front was an APC and could go anywhere. Off we went with me staring goggle eyed at the light in front when, after half an hour, the tiny light suddenly disappeared. The APC had gone down a steep bank resembling the Grand Canyon in the dark. "Still want me to follow, Sir?" I asked politely knowing it would be impossible. "Don't talk like an idiot!" he retorted. To be fair, he started it.

After taking a wide detour we eventually arrived at our new location. The road sat on a ridge with the rifle company on one side and us on the other. The fact that the road and the ridge were between us would prove to be a blessing during the course of the night. On the opposite side of the ridge the rifle company had formed their vehicles up in a league, all the vehicles in three rows so that the ration truck, the ammo truck and the fuel pod could drive up and down replenishing them. The Battalion had done this hundreds of times without incident. But this wasn't one of those times. The refuelling vehicle sat in the middle of the three columns and began filling up one of the APCs when, for some unknown reason, it suddenly ignited! Having a blazing fuel pod amongst you wasn't a healthy thing so all the remaining vehicles shot off in all directions leaving the fuel pod and a burning APC. Just to complicate matters the blazing APC had taken on ammunition for the following day's live shoot! We were relatively safe on our side of the road and the ridge but it sounded like the mother of all battles taking place on the other side. There were bangs and flashes galore with the occasional 84mm round going off. Our snoring friend didn't have to keep us awake that night. I heard that the whole conflagration cost in excess of £1,000,000. You expect some damage on exercise but that was ridiculous. Some poor Major General in Whitehall must have had a heart attack and fell on his rattling medals when he got the bill for that.

Because of the cold nights I was still suffering from the dreaded 'white finger' so I paid a visit to the medical centre. I showed the medic my dead digit and after some deliberation he took a needle and told me to put my hand behind my back. "Can you feel that?" he asked me as he prodded my finger with the needle. Yes, I could feel a blunt prodding. But he was prodding with the sharp end! "It's your circulation," he concluded and sent me away before my nasty finger fell onto his nice clean floor.

Following that we all had R&R and I spent it with my crew in Wainwright and had a great time. I did telephone the Clark family in Lone Rock but they had gone to Saskatoon for their son's wedding. Wedding? If I had known that I would have packed my best jeans! Then it was a bus ride to Edmonton and a long flight back to Germany. Although we had a shit tour this time I still loved Canada. I might go back one day.

Chapter 23   On the Piste

There's a lot been said about the RSM, Mickey Wish, but I found him a very agreeable man. He could have had me shot on many occasions. The first was when I was guard commander and I was sitting at the desk having a chat with some of the lads. When the chat dried up I picked up the un-ringing phone and said into the mouthpiece, by way of a laugh, "Battersea dogs home!" I was absolutely astonished when the RSM appeared on the line and said "Who's that?" What were the chances of the RSM dialling the gate house when I picked up the phone!? Even though I was there and it was me that did it, I still can't believe it. Another time I was on night duty as the Company Orderly Sergeant in the company office. It wasn't unknown for the COS to pop across to the mess and have a few beers, we just had to let the guardroom know where we were. Unfortunately I met a mate of mine in there who had just been promoted. Well I couldn't let that pass without celebrating! After drinking far too many beers for a soldier on duty I crawled back to the company office and slid into my sleeping bag. However some high flying officer decided on a call out, not a big one, just a call out to get the men paraded on the square. I went round and woke up the soldiers but found one missing. I don't recall his name but it was a name you would have found difficult to pronounce when you were sober let alone after a few beers. The companies paraded and the COS of each company would march up to the RSM and check them in as present and correct. Except me. I marched up to the RSM. "Company present and correct except for...." and slurred the difficult moniker.

"HQ Company pleasant and erect Sir ..."

The RSM leaned towards me. "Who?" he asked. Again I cocked up the pronunciation. "How many beers have you had Corporal Russell?" he enquired. "One Sir!" I replied. He looked at me, clearly not believing it. "How many?" he asked, stepping closer. "Two Sir!" I said, hoping that would appease him. "See me in my office in the morning," he said casually and walked away. I went back to the company office and was met by the Company Sergeant Major. "You fuckin' twat!" he said, "I'd already told the RSM that the company was present and correct!! Then you walk up, pissed as a fart, and tell him someone is missing!?" Apparently the missing soldier wasn't missing at all. Next morning, I stood outside the RSMs office saying a fond farewell to my stripes. I marched in and stamped in at the brass strip in front of his desk. The RSM got up out of his seat and stared out of the window. "How many beers did you have last night Corporal Russell?" he asked. "Three Sir," I said. "We're both men of the world," he said quietly, "and we both know the rules." He turned from the window and looked at me. "You do know you're not supposed to drink on duty don't you?" Of course I did but before I could answer he fixed me with a nailing glare. "Think about it before you answer," he said. I did think about it. "Yes Sir," I told him. He went back to the window probably wondering how he could get a firing squad together. Then he turned to me again. "Have you seen the colours boards that L/Cpl Offer is working on?" he asked. "I have Sir," I said, "they're looking pretty good." He then told me that Taffy Offer was off sick at the moment. "I want you in the workshop finishing them." He said. "There's still quite some work involved..." "I want them finished." His tone told me that he wanted them finished. Then he dismissed me. Whatever anyone says about Mickey Wish he didn't do me any harm.

I was busy scribbling away on my drawing board in the office when I was summoned by the 2i/c. There was nothing unusual about that so I grabbed a notebook and pen and went to his office. I tapped on the door and went in. Major Shepherd sat behind his desk. "You called for me Sir?" I said. Normally he would invite me to take a seat at this point but he omitted to this time. "Ah yes, Corporal Russell," he said, "Well I've been looking at your records and I can see how you became a Corporal." I looked at him with a quizzical squint. "If I had my way," he continued, "you would still be a Private." I was so stunned I couldn't think of an immediate reply. To be honest I didn't think he was much of an Officer but I wouldn't be that rude to tell him so. He then went on to fire me from the Int Section and told me to report to the QMs in the morning. "Dismissed!" he said, as if to seal the deal. I was dumbfounded, I know I'd upset the old fart but I was good at my job. Nobody could believe it. If the Major did have a sense of humour, he concealed it very skilfully.

Next morning I reported to the QMs as instructed and they put me in the workshop. Meanwhile the Int Section lost a draughtsman, an APC driver and their NBC NCO all in one blow. Did they miss me? I'll never know, it seemed that all contact had been broken off. I know Captain Waller missed me. He approached me when I was walking through the camp. "Corporal Russell!" he called, "I've got a job for you." It was a job for a draughtsman. I apologised to the good Captain and explained that I no longer worked in the Int Section because the 2i/c had fired me. "You're joking!" he said in disbelief, "We'll see about that!" then he marched off in the direction of the HQ building. But even Captain Waller, with all his tact and diplomacy, could pull no strings. Corporal Russell was well and truly ostracised and, as far as TAC HQ were concerned, I never existed.

The lads in the workshop were great but I didn't feel that I belonged there. I'd been there before and it was different then, I first went there on my terms not those of the 2i/c. Maybe next time I have a laugh with a senior Officer I'll do it when he's not listening. It was in the workshop where I met a young lad. (Again his name escapes me, something like 'Julian') He was a nice young lad and was on work experience with us. He was smart and well-spoken and I got on well with him, even though I would take the piss out of his posh intonation. "I'm popping orf for luncheon then John," he would say. "Tootle pip then old bean, enjoy the Pimms!" said I. The Pimms became quiet prominent in our exchanges and he asked me if I'd ever tried one. "Nah," I said, "I'm a beer man." Then, out of the blue, he invited me round to his dad's house for a Pimms! I thought that was very nice of him and, not being one to disappoint, I popped round to his dad's house one evening. But there was something he hadn't told me; his dad was a Colonel in a neighbouring regiment! Maybe I should have worn incompetent pants. As it happened I had absolutely nothing to worry about, he was a lovely man and we got on like a house on fire. No 'Sir' or 'Corporal' it was first name terms and we had a very interesting chat. And a few Pimms of course! If I had got on with Major Shepherd like that I'd be in the Officers Mess within a week! It was a wonderful night and I was sorry to see his lad leave at the end of his work experience.

July 1983

The only problem I had owning a car was I knew nothing about them, especially the engine bit. Having had a go at a nut on my rocker cover I chewed the bloody thing. I decided a visit to our REME blokes would be a good idea so I drove over to the MT yard. The Sergeant there was most helpful and extracted the offending bolt. While we were there, a military ambulance shot by towards the APC garages. "Another case of hatch rash," we both agreed. But it was worse than that. Next morning I walked into the workshop and was greeted by Barry Hemsley. "Have you heard about Captain Waller?" he said. "No. Why?" I asked him. "He got killed yesterday in the MT yard." I couldn't believe it, probably the best Officer I had the privilege of knowing and now he was dead? It was the result of a stupid accident with a new experimental vehicle in the yard. He died on 21st July 1983. Not only was he a superb Officer but I also saw him as a friend.

In the meantime, the Army rolled out hearing tests and I went along for my appointment. I didn't think I had a problem with my hearing apart from having the TV too loud, but apart from that I felt fine. The first appointment was somewhat primitive; I sat with my back to the doctor and listened to varying sounds through a set of headphones. If I heard a noise in my left ear then I would put up my left arm until the sound went away and the same with my right ear and arm. At one point I got a noise in my left ear and put my arm up. The noise seemed to stay there so my arm was still raised when the doctor came round to the front of me. "Do you want the toilet?" he asked. Apparently I had tinnitus. So they sent me to the Military Hospital in Hannover where they put me in a soundproofed box. Whenever I heard a noise I would press a red button. Being in the soundproofed box made me more aware of the tinnitus, so when I emerged I told the medic. "I had a noise like a distant waterfall in my left ear," I said. "That's just the sound of silence" he replied. "Could you look at my right ear then," I asked him, "because I couldn't hear it in that one." So it came to pass that, at the tender age of 29 years, I was a deaf old fart.

"Pardon?"
(Testing the Mk 1 improvised hearing aid)

August 1983

Walking past the Company Office one day, the Company Sergeant Major stopped me and pointed to the notice board. 'Barman wanted', the notice said, 'Silberhutte Ski Training School'. "That'll be nice for someone Sir," I remarked. "Indeed it would," he said, "Pack your bags, you're going." Had I missed something? "But Sir," I protested, "It's clearly asking for a volunteer!" "Well volunteered," he said, "now pack your bags." Well, it seems the Army did have a sense of humour tucked away after all. They were sending me as a barman?! So I did pack my bags, said goodbye to the family and headed south to the mountains.

I arrived at Silberhutte and it was a very picturesque vision of snowy mountains and pine forests. Hardly the place you would expect to find something belonging to the Army. The ski school was a small place which housed the accommodation, stores, cinema and 3 bars. The Senior Ranks bar was probably the most comfortable while the students bar was almost like a canteen. Then there was the permanent staff bar, a shit hole of a dungeon in the basement. Guess which one I got. The permanent staff were a fine bunch which also included some local staff. We had a variety of tables and chairs that were probably donated by the local slum and a tabletop football game with a player missing. It was certainly cold down there but we kept warm by burning students who strayed down there in error. It quickly dawned on me that this was nothing less than a retirement home for unwanted soldiers; we were all misfits for one reason or another.

One of the permanent staff I met was Graham, the camp projectionist, a stocky Northern bloke. He was actually a ski instructor but, prior to my arrival, he was involved in an accident with a Bedford truck. He was in the back of it when it went off the road and the tow bar hit him on the head, so he was advised not to ski. Being a lover of films, I soon became his best mate. Because he was a lover of beer, and the projectionist, we became firm friends. He quickly realised that if he bought me a few beers there was the likelihood of a stay back after hours. This was a reciprocal arrangement because if he had a decent film on the reel we would take a few beers in the cinema and watch the film after the bar closed. We shared the same sense of humour so 'Sherlock Holmes' Smarter Brother' and 'Airplane' were top of our list. Much better than 'The Apple Dumpling Gang'.

We had a Sergeant Major there who would do the stock take every morning. He would come into my grotty bar and look at the optics. "How many tots do you reckon are in there?" he asked, pointing at the whisky bottle. I'd peer at it and guess 6 or 7. "Only one way to be sure." He said and placed a glass under the optic and poured 6 tots. "Now," he said, looking at it with a watery eye, "we can either put it back in the bottle or drink it." "That's entirely up to you Sir," I said. So he drank it. "That's easier than getting it back in the bottle!" he said wisely. The daily stock checks became weekly. The Sergeant Major was probably told to cut down on his drinking.

We shared our bar with a family of mice, a rather large family by the look of it, so we got some mouse traps from the stores and set them up around the bar. They were the old spring traps, the eager sort that snapped your fingers before catching anything. But they worked and one morning we found a furry victim in one of them. Some of the local staff were always playing on the tabletop football and they thought he would make an excellent stand-in for the missing player. They tied his tail to the bar but, after a few games, the mouse transferred into the goal and was never seen again. These German locals would always appear at lunchtime. "Alles Klar!" they would say. I asked them who 'Alice Clark' was but they just laughed.

The stay backs would continue after hours and rather than sit in the dingy bar, we sat behind it. Seats were at a premium so we sat on whatever was available. One night Graham chose to sit on the Carlsberg barrel with the rest of us squatting where we could. We chatted away quietly because we didn't want those in the Senior Staff bar to hear us. Then someone looked behind Graham and questioned the position of the valve, he thought it had moved. Graham said it was already like that when he sat down so we carried on waffling. The waffle stopped when the valve on the Carlsberg barrel shot off sending a shower of lager up Graham's back like an alcoholic tsunami. We probably made more noise throwing ourselves on the barrel than the escaping gas and beer. We just pissed ourselves laughing, with Graham laughing until his shirt dried out.

"Quick! Grab some glasses!!"
(Graham and his Carlsberg tsunami)

After a while we heard that our stock taking Sergeant Major was leaving us, he was being returned to his unit for some reason... The senior bar staff decided they would go out on the town with him and give him a send-off and they asked if I could pick them up at the end of the night. Why not? I drove up the snow covered road to the town and they all clambered aboard and I transported them back to the ski school. The Sergeant Major, being completely rat arsed, decided he wanted one last drink in his mess bar. So one of the staff managed to procure the keys from the guardroom and we all went into the posh bar and had a few beers in comfort. The Sergeant Major said he knew about our stay backs (he could hear the laughing) but he didn't give a monkeys. He sat at the bar and looked at all of the regimental plaques that adorned the walls and then he picked up an ornamental ice pick and attacked them! Obviously we couldn't let that happen so we restrained him, calmed him down and put him to bed. I'd like to think we saved him a lot of shit in the morning. My time at Silberhutte was coming to a close and I had the final stock take in my grubby old bar. It was 200 deutschmarks down, about £50! How did that happen? Probably someone not playing the game on those notorious stay backs. Never trust a drunk!

When I got home, Pam and the boys were leaving me. Nothing permanent, she was heading back to Coventry to take over the house we would be living in when I left the Army, which was only a matter of weeks away. I stayed behind and my first job was to hand the quarter over with everything pristine and clean, even the black enamelled hobs on the cooker. Then the Officer marching us out came to inspect. The hobs were the first things he noticed. He told me they should be copper coloured. Well bless my socks, they were black when we moved in. "Soak them in vinegar," he advised. By the time I moved back into barracks they were a nice shiny copper colour.

January 1984

When I moved back into the barracks I had a bunk all to myself, not like those shared rooms I lived in all those years before. But that presented me with a problem; I was never any good at getting up in the morning. Pam always woke me up and prior to that everyone else in the room used to get me up. So on those occasions when I did oversleep I would tootle off to the Medical Centre on the pretence of an appointment regarding my hearing. But Sergeant Major 'Spunky' Moss was acting RSM and he only fell for that one so many times. One day he felt I had pushed my luck so he put me on a charge. I was double marched into the OCs office where Captain Broomfield was acting CO. (Most of the battalion was away training for Northern Ireland so we had lots of people holding acting ranks.) The Captain had a blue fit. "How do you expect soldiers in Northern Ireland to follow your command if you can't even get up in the morning!?" he bellowed. It was a good point and I didn't want to interrupt him. "Being an NCO you should be setting an example! You really should think about your future with the battalion Corporal Russell!" "I'm leaving in two weeks Sir," I told him. "What!?? Leaving for where?!" he asked. "Leaving the Army Sir." Suddenly the exploding Officer went all calm, like a volcano that had run out of lava. "Well good luck in Civvy Street, Corporal Russell," he said and shook my hand. 'Spunky' Moss marched me out of the office and developed a noticeable twitch.

With most of the Battalion away on training we were essentially the rear party, looking after the camp and doing guard duties on a night on / night off basis. With it getting closer and closer to my departure I spent most of my free nights visiting people to say goodbye. One night there was a terrific wind blowing, taking down trees and blowing the puttees off the less experienced squaddy. It was howling. I'd already had a skin full in the mess when I decided to see Brian and Pat Clarke on the Interbau Estate. After all, it was only a short drive away. As I hit the road to the Interbau Estate I saw blue lights in my rear view mirror, the Military Police. Bollocks, what a way to end my career. I didn't pull over immediately but carried on into the estate car park. The blue lights had disappeared and for a moment I thought how lucky I was. Maybe the wind blew the Land Rover off the road! As I got out of the car, an MP stepped through the bushes. "Hello," he said, trying to stand up straight in the wind, "Do you know what a blue light means?" I clung to my car door because of the wind, which kindly blew my beery breath away to some unknown place. "I thought you were attending an incident and were trying to pass," I said. "Yeah, we noticed you were trying to pull to the side," he said. Pull to the side? I was trying to keep the car on the road! Then he told me it was just a routine documents check so I got them out of the glove box and presented them to him. "Lovely night for it," I said as my beery breath whipped across the road. "Have a good evening," he said as he handed me my documents back. Was he kidding? There I was, clinging to my door in a gale with my skin billowing like a baggy body stocking, and he says 'have a good evening'? But at least he didn't breathalyse me so I forgave him.

Next morning I was strolling through the corridor of the QMs department when a lieutenant called out to me. I know he was calling me because there was only me and him in the corridor, but with my deafness and the echo I couldn't hear what he was saying. "Sorry Sir?" I said as I made my way towards him. He repeated himself but I still couldn't make out what it was. "Sorry Sir," I said as I approached him, "I couldn't hear what you were saying." "Are you fackin' deaf or what!?" he ranted, so I produced the medical chit from my pocket and showed him. "Oh, terribly sorry Corporal," he said politely. We went down the steps as he repeated, yet again, what he had said and I saw a familiar figure coming up towards us. "Hello John mate!" he said and shook my hand. It was John Burke who I had known previously from the orderly room, but now he was sporting the pips of a lieutenant on his epaulettes! "Hello John," I said, "how are you?" Well, Lieutenant Burke and Corporal Russell had a right old chat on the stairs. I've no idea what the other Officer was thinking but, then again, we didn't ask. That was a nice reunion.

Well, just when I found a friend in a high place, I had two days left and one guard duty. But why? I had my ticket, the car was fuelled up and my paperwork was complete. What was I waiting for? Mind you, if I didn't do my duty then my mate Chris Drake would end up doing it. Without another thought I drove through the barrier of St Barbara Barracks one last time and headed off to Zeebruge. After hours of driving I reached the port and boarded the Herald of Free Enterprise ferry. I was surprised Spunky Moss hadn't sent his Regimental Policemen there to meet me; they probably hadn't missed me yet. (Years later I would come across Chris. He throttled me.)

The following day I was reunited with Pam and the boys in Coventry where, 12 years earlier, it had all began. We spent a few weeks sorting things out then I had to pay one final visit to Bassingbourn for my pre-release medical. It was odd driving into Bassingbourn Barracks after all those years and even stranger when I booked into the guardroom where I was incarcerated 10 years previously. At the Medical Centre they put me in a soundproofed box for a hearing test. "But I'm deaf as a post," I told them, but they put me in anyway. I spent a good half hour listening and pressing a button. The medic turned up to let me out. "The test finished ten minutes ago," he said then looked at the print out. "Good lord!" he exclaimed, "You're as deaf as a post!" Isn't that what I told him? Then he wanted a urine sample. Why not, the Army had been taking the piss for years, once more wouldn't hurt. But my water works wouldn't play so the medic stood me by the sink and ran the taps. "Never fails," he said. But it did fail and I still didn't want to go. My bladder finally relented after two pints of water down my neck. After being entertained by the medical staff I returned to my car which was parked outside the HQ building. As I got my keys out one of the guard approached me. "The RSM wants a word with you Sir," he told me. Oh dear, maybe the Army wanted their 24 hours back because I left early. Would I have the same cell in the guardroom? The sentry escorted me to the RSMs office and I marched in. "Ah!" he said, "So it's your car outside my building! Where are you from?" I told him who I was and where I was from. I also told him I was there for my pre-release medical. "3 Queen's," he said, "You'll know my good friend Barry Moss then!" I told him that I did indeed know 'Spunky' Moss and rather expected him to say "he wants you locking up for being AWOL." But he didn't. Instead we had a very pleasant chat about the Army in general, and then he shook my hand and wished me luck. Nice bloke whoever he was. As I returned to my car I bumped into my old friend Martin Lyons who had been posted to Bassingbourn on the training staff. It wouldn't do to see an old mate and not have a drink so we went to the NAAFI and had a few beers. With two pints of water and two pints of beer inside me it was hell driving home. With my bladder at full capacity I felt like I was sitting astride a space-hopper…

And finally....

If I had my time again would I join the Army? Definitely. Would I join the same southern regiment? Absolutely. Would I make the same mistakes? Probably! The Army isn't for everyone and, at times, I felt it wasn't for me in the early days. Bill Dixon summed it up when he told me "You're not really a soldier, you're Civvy attached!" But it was great experience. If I had stayed in Civvy Street I would never have seen the Northern Lights in Canada or the Lower St. Michael's Cave in Gibraltar. I certainly wouldn't have visited the countries I did and, more importantly, I would never have met the wonderful people that I did. People like Norman and Molly Clark and their family in Lone Rock, or Alma in Belize. I joined the Army as a boy and it made a man out of me, teaching me what responsibility is and to take pride in everything I do. It's a world where great responsibility is thrust upon 18 year olds, and some of those 18 year olds made the ultimate sacrifice, laying down their lives for their country. Nobody else in any other walk of life would, or could, push themselves that far. And yet young lads still join the Army and tread the same path even though they faced Iraq and Afghanistan. (My youngest son, John junior, wasn't mentioned in the book because he wasn't born until after I left the Army. But he joined at 18 and, I'm proud to say, he served his time in the Gulf and Afghanistan. I look forward to his retrospective diary!)

Although I dedicated this book to my mum and dad, I also dedicate it to all those soldiers who served before me, alongside me, and those who have followed since. Somebody once said "If you can read this thank a teacher. If you're reading it in English then thank a soldier." How true. Meanwhile I espy someone in need of company, I'll just grab a sandbag and take this hurricane lamp across...

Dave Cole, Myself and Pam
The Queen's Regiment Memorial
National Memorial Arboretum
15th May 2016

(Photo courtesy of Tony Cole)

Some other cartoons from those days ...

"DONT WORRY ABOUT IT MATE — ALL IS NORMAL!"

'O.P. BURBERRY.'

"... Sgt Dixon made a name for himself..."

"DUE TO UNFORSEEN CIRCUMSTANCES WE SHALL NOW GO ONTO ACCESS PLATES & PLUGS...."

(THE 3 WISE MONKEY'S — ALTCAR CAMP 1977.)

WE'RE NOT LOST JENKINS... WE'RE MERELY GEOGRAPHICALLY DISORIENTATED.
NOW PASS ME THAT THINGY WITH THE NORTH & WOTSIT SPIN AROUND THING...
RUPERT

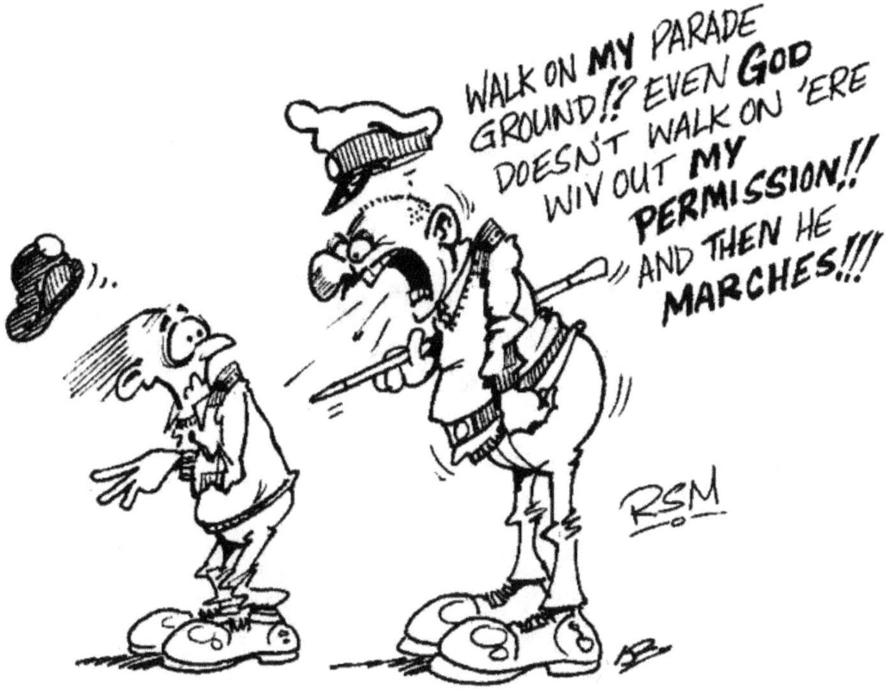
WALK ON MY PARADE GROUND!? EVEN GOD DOESN'T WALK ON 'ERE WIV OUT MY PERMISSION!! AND THEN HE MARCHES!!!
RSM

PUT YOUR SKIDS BACK ON FRED, THEY'VE GONE!

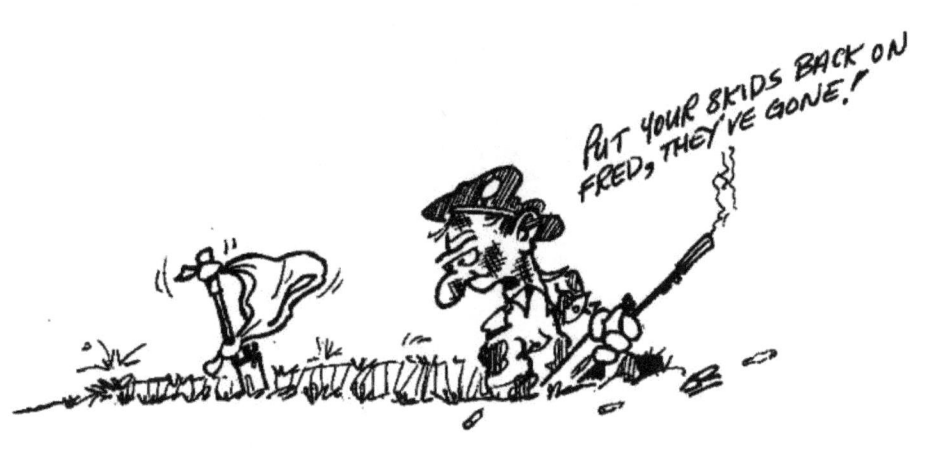

"...Then both ends of the frame met in the middle..."

And some pictures ...

Me in the Drummer Boy pub, Tidworth, 1972

Me with Sergeant John Riley (REME)
St. George's Caye, Belize.

San Pedro, Belize.

Bessbrook, Northern Ireland

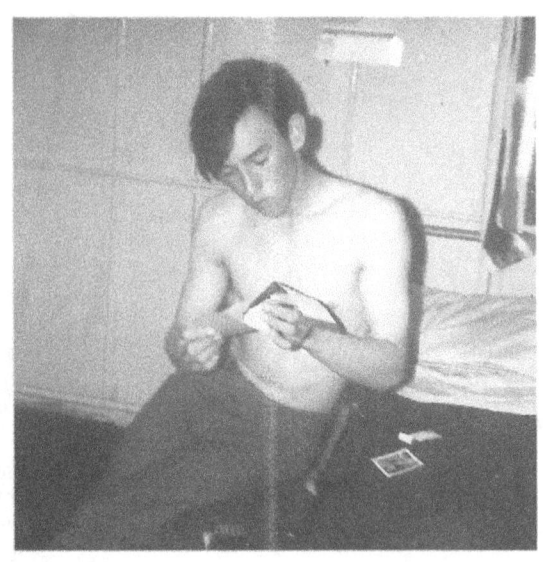

Sherriff checking the breakfast menu, Bassingbourn.

On the ranges, Dover.

Danger! Cartoonist at work, Dover

With the Signals Platoon, Italy

Catching lizards, San Pedro, Belize

QMs Department. Gibraltar

15 ton mess tin, the 432 AFV. Borden. (Chapter 20)

Captain Fitzgerald (MO), Sergeant Sinden, Alan Richards
And L/Cpl Scouse Giman (RAMC).
Medical Centre, Cyprus. (Chapter 9)

Me and Pam, Connaught Barracks, Dover. (Chapter 17)

Steve Terry, John Docherty, Trevor Francis, Me, Bob Tufnel,
Bill Kempton, Chris Gheratty. Piggery Ridge, Londonderry, N.I.
(Chapter 6)

Me, Sergeant Mike Sinden and N/K. Medical Centre, Cyprus. (Chapter 9)

www.ingramcontent.com/pod-product-compliance
Lightning Source LLC
Chambersburg PA
CBHW062158080426
42734CB00010B/1739